Doing Social Research

A Guide to Coursework

Peter Langley

cartoons by Allan Cubitt

Causeway Books

Causeway Press Ltd
PO Box 13, Ormskirk, Lancashire L39 5HP
© Causeway Press Ltd, 1987
1st Impression 1987
Reprinted 1987, 1988

British Library Cataloguing in Publication Data
Langley, Peter
    Doing social research: a guide to
    coursework
    1. Social sciences — Methodology
    I. Title
    300'.72   H61

    ISBN 0-946183-29-5

Phototypesetting by Franklyn Graphics, Formby, Merseyside
Printed and bound in England by Alden Press Ltd., Oxford, England

CONTENTS

Acknowledgements

The author would like to thank the following pupils of John Ruskin High School, Croydon for permission to use their work.

Louise Brickley
Abigail Bridgeman
Alison Bulled
Gaby Campbell
Elenie Card
Lisa Copsey
Jan De-Iulio
Neill Gardiner
Stephen Grace
Julie Harris
Ruth Hemsley
Kamlesh Lakhani
Sharon Maia

Dan McHale
Joanne Newland
Priti Patel
Lisa Riordan
Helen Rowlerson
Andrew Schendel
Karen Sheridan
Kellie Simmons
Maria Straw
Jenny Tillotson
Susan Tolley
Joanne Whitmore

We are grateful to the following for permission to reproduce copyright material (details in text).

The Controller of Her Majesty's Stationery Office for table p. 45 and graph p. 46.
Social and Community Planning Research for extracts from questionnaires pp. 11 and 12.
Yaffa Character Licensing for cartoon p. 78.

Every effort has been made to locate the copyright owners of material quoted in the text. Any omissions brought to our attention are regretted and will be credited in subsequent printings.

Teacher's Introduction

This book is not a textbook on research methods but a practical guide for pupils on how to do their own social research. It is designed to provide guidance on every aspect, and at every stage, of the coursework component of GCSE Sociology and Social Science courses, whether the coursework consists of one project using a variety of methods, or two or more shorter projects using one method. The book includes step-by-step guides on how to use each of the main methods of data collection.

The text is interspersed with a large number of short exercises which aim to test pupils' ability to apply the ideas in the book to the kind of research situations they are likely to encounter. These can be set as written work, discussed in class, or worked through by students individually or in groups. Each section also contains cartoons and quotations from pupils' own research. These aim to provoke discussion as well as amusement.

It is hoped that the book can be used in a variety of ways: read through and discussed in class rather like a traditional textbook; issued to pupils to work through at their own pace; or 'dipped into' by students whenever they need help with a particular aspect of their coursework.

1 Why Do Social Research?

'The poor are lazy – that's why they're poor.'
'You can't blame the poor for being poor; it's not their fault.'

'Many people who get divorced don't take marriage seriously.'
'Many people who stay married don't take marriage seriously.'

'Britain is a divided country.'
'Class isn't important anymore.'

How do you know which of these statements is right and which wrong?

It's just common sense, isn't it?

Each of us knows a great deal about the things social scientists are always telling us about like the family, education, and the mass media. Why should their views and their explanations be any better than our own 'common sense' ideas?

That's a complicated question, but one reason why this might be the case is that social scientists have spent years doing research, collecting evidence as carefully and as scientifically as they can. This means that they are likely to have a clearer picture of society as a whole. We tend to base our views of society on our own and our friends' and relations' experiences. This is likely to be a rather narrow view.

> Example: You have an uncle who started off his career in a very low position and has now become the firm's managing director. This may lead you to believe that his kind of achievement is quite common as long as someone has the talent and makes the effort. However, sociologists who have spent years studying movement between social classes will tell you that what has happened to your uncle is very rare, and that many hard working and talented people never improve their position at work.

Many of the beliefs we hold are based on prejudice. This means that they are biased. An obvious example is racial prejudice. Many people have negative views of ethnic minorities when they have never even met members of these groups. Their beliefs are not based on solid information. Social research can provide information on which to base an **objective**, or unbiased, view. In addition, most social scientists do their best to prevent

1

their own bias and prejudice from influencing their research. Try to do the same in your coursework. Keep an open mind – it's difficult but it's the only way to get near the truth. Doing research won't necessarily tell you which of the quotes at the beginning of this section are true, but it will give you some information on which to base an opinion.

During your coursework you will be able to collect evidence which should give you a much clearer and more accurate view of whatever you are studying than that held by the vast majority of people. The more evidence you collect, and the more carefully you collect it, the more accurate your results will probably be. Don't expect to find out anything very startling though; in most cases the examiners are more interested in how you go about doing your research than in the results you end up with. Your research could be a complete disaster but you could still end up with a top grade if you clearly describe all the problems you had and show what you have learned from them.

The more your coursework focuses on local topics the more original your findings are likely to be. You should take other social scientists' work into account, but basically what you discover will be unique to you. This is a chance for you to find out about the social world for yourself without relying on what teachers or textbooks tell you. It's a great opportunity – enjoy it. This book should give you some help.

2 Starting Research

You are probably following a course in Sociology or Social Science. Your research should, therefore, be concerned with testing and examining some of the ideas from these subjects. Look at Section 15 for some examples.

How do I choose what to study?

Example

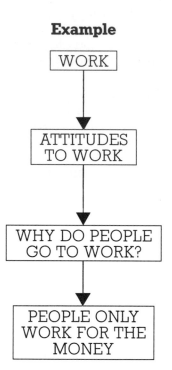

1. Find a general area of the subject that you're interested in. You can do this by:-
   – looking through your notes
   – looking through textbooks.

2. This area is likely to be too general to successfully research so you need to narrow it down further. Find a particular aspect of the area you have chosen which you would like to concentrate on.

3. This topic is probably still too wide to base research on. Focus on one question or problem which you would like to investigate in more detail.

4. Turn this question or problem into an **hypothesis**. An hypothesis is a possible answer to, or explanation of, a question. You should develop an hypothesis which you think might be true and use your research to try and find out whether or not it is. In terms of the example on the right you would test whether or not it is true that people only work for money.

Exercise 1

Try to create hypotheses from these questions:–
a) What do young people think of the police?
b) Why do so many 18 and 19 year olds choose not to vote in elections?
c) What are 'football hooligans' really like?
d) Why do the mass media pay so much attention to drug abuse?

4

Do I have to use an hypothesis?

Using an hypothesis gives your coursework a clear aim and helps you keep to the point. However, you don't have to use one. In some cases they are not necessary – when you simply want to find out more about something for instance. Another possibility is to develop a hypothesis as your research progresses and you discover more about the topic under investigation. Many professional researchers do not use hypotheses, and many who do either change or reject them over the course of their research. Be prepared for this to happen during your coursework.

Hints on choosing a research project

Do choose something you're interested in. Your coursework is likely to take up quite a lot of time. If you're not interested in it you won't want to work hard on your own.

Do choose something that is relevant to the subject. Topics such as the life story of your pet alligator are to be avoided!

Do choose something that it is possible to find out about. You may be very interested in how many of your teachers had sex before marriage but it is unlikely that you will be able to find out.

Do choose something you already know a little about. You could focus your research on an aspect of your local area, your peer group, or a club you belong to. This is likely to make your results more original.

Do choose a research project you can relate to.

Don't choose a topic just because your friend has chosen it. This may well lead to you becoming very bored.

Don't write 'all I know' about the topic. Use your hypothesis or a clear set of aims to focus your research.

Exercise 2

Think about the following hypotheses. State the advantages and disadvantages of using each as the basis for your own coursework.
a) Being young and unemployed is not as stressful as being middle aged and unemployed.
b) China's policy of one child per family produces spoiled brats.
c) Fewer girls than boys study Physics because it is considered a 'boys' subject'.
d) Most young people have similar attitudes to their parents – the 'generation gap' does not exist.

How should I start my research?

You might want to start by having a look at textbooks and other books relevant to your coursework. These should give you ideas about:
- the work other social scientists have done on the topic
- the method or methods which you could use
- the **concepts** (words or phrases developed to help understand something) which might be important in your research. Example 1 on p. 86 and Example 5 on p. 92 show how you might use concepts such as age, class, and ethnic group in your research.

The next stage is to decide how you are going to collect **data** – information.

The next eight sections of the book explain which methods of data collection are available to you and how you can use them. Section 11 deals with choosing the methods most useful for your research.

What's starting research really like?

'I chose the topic of roles in marriage because a lot of the work we did in class showed that roles were being shared more but, looking at the married couples I knew, I didn't believe this was true.'

'I chose this topic because I'm interested in a career in nursing and thought that studying health would teach me more about it.'

'I chose to study "Girls and Sport" because I was puzzled at the lack of girls at BMX meetings.'

'People often call me a snob so I decided to do my coursework on social class.'

'I tried to choose something simple so I wouldn't confuse myself.'

'I realised that doing research on just racism was too wide so I narrowed it down to the attitudes of different generations to racism.'

'My hypothesis was ''People still believe in traditional sex roles''. I wanted to see whether this was true. I thought I would keep referring back to it so I wouldn't lose track of what I was doing. However, I found this difficult and sometimes forgot about it.'

'When I started I did not set out to prove or disprove anything – I had no hypothesis.'

Primary Sources

Primary data is information you collect yourself. When you use primary sources of data:-

- Collect the data as carefully as you can; even little mistakes can make your results incorrect.

- Try to be **objective** when collecting data. This means not letting your views influence the way you do the research.

  The following four sections deal with methods of collecting and using primary data.

3 Questionnaires

What is a questionnaire?

A questionnaire is simply a list of questions. There are two ways of answering them:-

1. The questions can be read to the respondent – the person answering – by an interviewer who ticks off or writes down their answers. This is called a **structured interview**.
2. The questionnaire can be given to the respondent who fills it in and the researcher collects it later. Or it can be sent and returned by post in which case it is known as a postal questionnaire.

Why use questionnaires?

- Questionnaires allow data to be collected from a large number of people.

- Questionnaires make it possible to compare respondents' answers to questions.

- Questionnaires are normally used to collect data which can be expressed in statistical form using graphs and tables. They are not very useful if you want very detailed information about respondents' attitudes, especially if you are asking questions about sensitive issues such as racism or divorce. In these cases in-depth interviews might be more effective.

- If you collect data from a large enough number of people who are a representative cross-section of a wider population then you can make statistical statements about that population e.g. 24% of households own or rent a video recorder. Pieces of research which aim to make these kinds of statements are called **social surveys**.

Which should I use: questionnaire or structured interview?

	Advantages	Disadvantages
Questionnaire	– large number of respondents possible	– possibility of low response rate (not getting many back)
	– respondent has time to consider questions	– questions cannot be explained to respondent

	Advantages	**Disadvantages**
Structured interview	– interviewer can explain questions to respondent and ask for more detail if necessary	– manner and appearance of interviewer can affect answers. For a detailed discussion of this see pages 25–26.

Exercise 1

a) Why might you want your sample (the people answering your questionnaire) to be as large as possible?
b) What steps could you take to avoid a low response rate for questionnaires you have given out?

Exercise 2

Look at the following cartoon of a researcher attempting to conduct an interview. Why do you think this interview might not have been very successful? What other situations can you think of where interviews might not be successful?

How do I write questions?

Extract from a questionnaire using an interviewer. The words in capital letters are instructions to the interviewer.

		Col./Code
	SECTION ONE	
1.	a) Do you normally read any daily morning newspaper at least 3 times a week?	**(148)**
	Yes	1
	No	2
	IF YES	
	b) Which one do you normally read? IF MORE THAN ONE ASK: Which one do you read *most* frequently? ONE CODE ONLY	**(149–50)**
	(Scottish) Daily Express	01
	Daily Mail	02
	Daily Mirror/Record	03
	Daily Star	04
	The Sun	05
	Daily Telegraph	06
	Financial Times	07
	The Guardian	08
	The Times	09
	Morning Star	10
	Other Scottish/Welsh/regional or local *daily* morning paper (SPECIFY)_____	11
	Other (SPECIFY)_____	12
	IF ANY PAPER NAMED	
	c) Suppose you saw or heard conflicting or different reports of the same news story on radio, television and in the ...... (PAPER NAMED AT Q1b). Which of the three versions do you think you would be *most* likely to believe ...... READ OUT	**(151)**
	...... the one on radio,	1
	the one on television,	2
	or – the one in the newspaper?	3
	(Don't know)	8
2.	Can you tell me where you usually get *most* of your news about what's going on in Britain today: is it from the newspapers, or radio, or television, or where?	**(152)**
	ONE CODE ONLY	
	Newspapers	1
	Radio	2
	Television	3
	Other (SPECIFY) _____	7
	Don't know	8

Source: *British Social Attitudes Survey, 1984,* Social and Community Planning Research

11

Extract from a questionnaire filled in by the respondents themselves. Notice how clear and simple the instructions are.

1. Please tick one box for *each* country below to show whether you think its *standard of living* is higher, about the same, or lower than Britain's.

PLEASE TICK ONE BOX ON EACH LINE

STANDARD OF LIVING

	Higher than Britain's	About the same as Britain's	Lower than Britain's
France	1	2	3
East Germany	1	2	3
West Germany	1	2	3
Japan	1	2	3
Canada	1	2	3
Australia	1	2	3

2. Now thinking of *influence on world events*. Please tick one box for *each* country below to show whether it generally has more influence, about the same amount of influence, or less influence than Britain has nowadays.

PLEASE TICK ONE BOX ON EACH LINE

INFLUENCE

	More than Britain	About the same amount as Britain	Less than Britain
France	1	2	3
China	1	2	3
East Germany	1	2	3
West Germany	1	2	3
Canada	1	2	3
Australia	1	2	3
Israel	1	2	3
India	1	2	3

Source: *British Social Attitudes Survey, 1984,* Social and Community Planning Research

- Work out exactly what you want to find out and only use questions which will help achieve this. What kinds of basic information do you need for instance: age, sex, class?

- Make your questions as simple and clear as possible, especially if the respondents are going to be completing the questionnaire on their own.

- Questions can be of two types:–

    Open: where a few lines are given to the respondent to fill in.
    Closed: where the respondent is given a number of alternative answers to choose from.

The advantage of open questions is that respondents can answer exactly how they want to; they are not forced to choose between your alternatives, as is the man in the cartoon below.

However, if the main purpose of your questionnaire is to produce statistics and graphs, you should use closed questions because they make it much easier to count up the different answers. This is made even easier if you give each alternative answer a number before you give the questionnaires out – this is called pre-coding. All the answers in the questionnaires on pages 11 and 12 are pre-coded.

There is a much better way of putting the closed question shown in the cartoon:–

What kind of dwelling do you live in?
1. House
2. Flat
3. Maisonette
4. Other (please specify) _____

Example of open question:-

What is your opinion of comprehensive schools?

_____

_____

● If you want to find out how strongly a respondent feels about something you can put the question in the following way:-

Please put a circle around the number of the answer that is closest to your view.

'The showing of violent incidents on television should be more strictly controlled.'
1. Strongly agree
2. Agree
3. Don't know
4. Disagree
5. Strongly disagree

Exercise 3

Here is an example of a very bad questionnaire. Make a list of all the things you can find wrong with it. It is to be completed by a random sample of women.

Name: _____

Address: _____

_____

Husband's job: _____

Husband's wage: _____

Does your husband help with housework?	Yes/No
How old are your children?	1–5
	5–10
	10–15
	15–20
Do your children often help you with housework?	Yes/No
Do you have joint conjugal roles?	Yes/No
You don't enjoy housework do you?	Yes/No

How do I choose who is going to answer my questionnaire?

It is not usually possible to give questionnaires to every person in the 'population' you're interested in, whether that 'population' is the pupils in your school, those living on a local estate, people who use a particular swimming pool, or the whole of Great Britain! This means that you will have to choose a smaller number of people to study. This smaller number is called your **sample**.

Your sample should reflect the population as a whole – it should be a cross-section. This allows you to say that the results you obtained from your sample probably apply to the whole of your population.

How do I choose a representative sample?

Example: Members of a Youth Club.

Method 1: Quota sample

- Observe the club at different times on the different days it is open.
- Note the age, sex and ethnic background of those using it.
- Your sample should include people in the same proportions (e.g. if 60% of members are female, 60% of your sample should be female).

Method 2: Stratified random sample

- Ask permission to look at a list of members of the club. A list of names to choose your sample from is called a **sampling frame**.
- As you want roughly equal numbers of each sex, make separate lists of girls and boys. This is called **stratifying** your sample.
- Give each name on the two lists a number.
- Choose a **random** sample from each list. A random sample is one based on pure chance, like drawing numbers out of a hat. Ask your Maths teacher for a table of random numbers and simply choose as many numbers as you want from this list.

Another method is to choose every third, fourth, or whatever, number on the lists. This is known as **systematic** sampling.

Exercise 5

Looking at the two methods of choosing a sample of members of a youth club, what might 'go wrong' with each method, causing you to end up with a sample which was not representative of users of the club?

What size should my sample be?

Your sample should not be so large that it is impossible to collect data from everyone in it, but large enough to accurately represent the population – a sample of 10 out of a population of 1000 is very unlikely to be representative, however carefully it is chosen!

Exercise 6

You want to give a questionnaire to a sample of 50 pupils at your school.
a) What could you use as a sampling frame?
b) How could you make sure that equal numbers of pupils from all year groups were included in your sample?

Exercise 7

How could you choose a representative sample of pupils at your school from ethnic minority backgrounds?

What do I do when all my questionnaires have been completed?

When you have finished interviewing or all your questionnaires have been returned, you will find that you have a large number of completed questionnaires. You need to transfer all this information on to one or two sheets of paper so that you can add up all the answers and turn them into statistics. At this point you will see how pre-coding has been useful. If your questionnaire was not pre-coded you must code it now. Even if it is pre-coded you will have to do some coding now:-

    – give each questionnaire a number
    – give each question a number
    – give each alternative answer a number

It is very hard to code open questions. These might be best used to draw attention to, or to illustrate, points you wish to make from the statistics.

You can now transfer all your results on to a few sheets of paper, as in the diagram opposite.

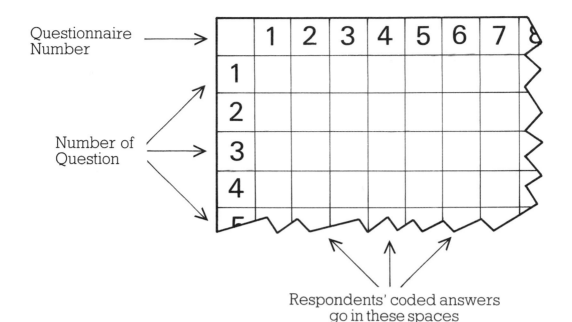

Questionnaire Number →

Number of Question →

Respondents' coded answers
go in these spaces

Once this chart is complete you can add up all the different answers to the questions, turn them into percentages if there are enough answers to make percentages mean anything, and draw line, bar, or pie graphs to show your results. You can find out about these different kinds of graphs on pp. 74–75. You may want to compare answers to two questions; e.g. how men and women answered one question. Make sure all your graphs are clearly labelled.

How to analyse questionnaire results

Q4 What kind of dwelling do
      you live in?
PLEASE TICK WHICH
ANSWER APPLIES TO YOU

1. House
2. Flat
3. Maisonette
4. Other (please specify)

_____

Pre-coded questionnaires filled in by respondent or interviewer.

17

- you have a pen, the questionnaire and something to lean on
- you do the interview in a private place
- you give the respondent all the necessary information about who you are and what you are doing
- you do each interview in the same way so that they can be compared, only changing the wording of questions if the respondent doesn't understand
- you don't influence the respondent's answers.

Warning: if you want to interview or give questionnaires to the 'general public', for instance interview in the street, you must check with your teacher first.

Make sure that the interview takes place at a convenient time for the respondent.

7. Collect all questionnaires in, code them, add up the answers and express them in statistical form. Make a note of the answers to open questions. Draw any graphs.

8. Write up the results of your questionnaire including:-

a) how you wrote the questionnaire and selected your sample

20

b) what your findings are: were any surprising; how did different groups of people answer questions differently; did your findings reflect the aims of your questionnaire?

c) problems you had doing the questionnaire: did you make any mistakes in sampling, writing the questions, collecting the questionnaires, doing the interviews?

d) how would you do the questionnaire differently if you did it again?

What's doing a questionnaire really like?

'I found some problems with adults. Some refused to fill my questionnaire in, and others rushed through it because they thought I was "just a school-kid".'

'I had a low response rate because I lost most of the questionnaires.'

'My questionnaire would have been more successful if I had made sure that older as well as younger people completed it.'

'I gave my questionnaire out during the school lunch hour. This meant that the boys filled it in in groups, twisting each question round to make a big joke out of it.'

'I could have got the information I wanted from official statistics – I think I just did a questionnaire because everyone else was.'

'Adding up all the answers took a long time and was really boring.'

'When I asked one person to fill in the questionnaire they said they were "too stoned" to do it at the moment. When they eventually filled it in they wrote that drugs do not affect their behaviour.'

'I chose to include some open questions so that respondents could write about their views.'

'One man I gave the questionnaire to decided he would like to sit down and talk to me about it as he had done 'A' level Sociology. He told me that my questions were too complicated and I got annoyed and swore at him. He complained to the school.'

'My first question was trying to find out whether the respondent was male or female. They had to fill in a blank space by the word "Sex". 58% of male respondents wrote "Yes please".'

Doing a questionnaire: reminders

Have you:-

- Thought whether a questionnaire could be effectively used in your research?

- Worked out the aims of your questionnaire: what are you trying to find out?

- Thought whether structured interviews or self-completion questionnaires are most useful to you?

- Taken great care in the wording of your questions and in the instructions to respondents?

- Taken great care in the choice of your sample?

- Made sure your respondents know who you are, what you are doing, and that their answers are confidential?

- Made careful arrangements for the collection of the questionnaires?

- Coded and analysed your results, drawing graphs where necessary?

- Written about your findings, quoting the answers to any open questions?

- Pointed out any problems you had and mistakes you made in doing the questionnaire?

4 In-depth Interviews

In-depth interviews are not as 'structured' as questionnaire interviews. They are more like 'chats', with the interviewer encouraging the respondent to give detailed answers and to express his or her views. Usually there is a list of topics to be covered and some particular questions to ask, although these questions are likely to be more general than those used in a structured interview.

Why use in-depth interviews?

Reasons why you might prefer in-depth to structured interviews in your research become clear when the two types of interview are compared.

Structured interview	In-depth interview
Advantages	**Disadvantages**
● Can reach a large sample	● Only a small number of these interviews can take place because each one can last for a long time
● Respondents' answers can be compared and then turned into statistical statements	● It is very difficult to compare directly the results of in-depth interviews because each interview is unique
● A representative sample can be selected and results used to make statements about the survey population (e.g. 78% of pupils at your school believe that school uniform should be abolished).	● Because your sample size is small your results are unlikely to be representative of a particular population.
Disadvantages	**Advantages**
● Respondents are 'forced' to choose between the alternative answers the interviewer gives them	● Respondents can answer questions in as much detail as they want

Disadvantages	**Advantages**
● It is difficult to obtain accurate data on attitudes, opinions and values	● Accurate information about respondents' attitudes, values and opinions can be obtained
● The respondent may feel inhibited and not be entirely honest	● The informal atmosphere encourages the respondent to be open and honest
● The interviewer has to stick to the questionnaire.	● The interviewer can adjust questions and change direction as the interview is taking place.

Structured interviews emphasise **reliability**: how accurately different respondents' answers can be compared.

In-depth interviews emphasise **validity**: how close answers get to the respondent's real views.

In practice interviews are often neither completely structured nor completely in-depth but somewhere between the two:-

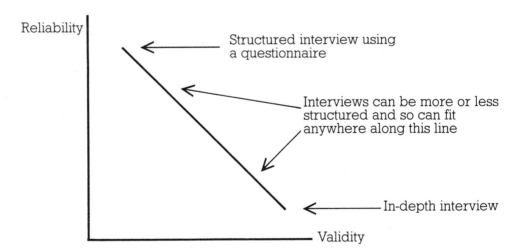

Exercise 1

Which kind of interview (structured or in-depth) do you think would be most useful in the investigation of the following. Give reasons for your answers.

a) How often people buy records
b) Why people like particular kinds of music
c) Young people's attitudes to religion
d) Older people's memories of the Second World War.

24

What affects the results of interviews?

Whatever you're 'really' like, your appearance can put people off.

The aim of any interview, whether structured or in-depth, is to collect accurate information from the respondent. Your interview results can be affected by your appearance and behaviour during the interview, as well as by the relationship you have with the respondent – and not just in the way shown in the cartoon on page 28!

● **Interviewer bias:** this occurs when the interviewer, either accidentally or deliberately, communicates his or her opinions to the respondent. This may cause the respondent simply to tell you what they think you want to hear. You must avoid asking 'leading' questions for example. These are questions which reveal the interviewer's opinions.

Examples:
'I think trade unions have too much power. What do you think?'

'Surely two children per family is enough?'

'You don't believe in life after death do you?'

Try not to put words into people's mouths. Remember, it's their opinions you want, not your own.

● The social status of the respondent and yourself can influence the results of an interview. You may be white or black, young or old, working class or middle class. These and other aspects of your social status may affect interview results.

Exercise 2

How might your social status affect the results of the following?

a) An interview with an elderly man about his experiences during the Second World War.
b) An interview with a black youth about his experiences of racism.
c) An interview with a labourer about work on a building site.
d) An interview with a mother about child rearing.
e) An interview with a male teenager about relations with the opposite sex.

- The results of your interview can also be affected by the personalities of the respondent and yourself. Interviews are rather like the conversations you have in everyday life. You might be shy or outgoing, chatty or quiet, aggressive or passive. In the same way your respondent will have various characteristics. These factors will influence the way the interview goes.

How can I use in-depth interviews?

- To provide detailed information about attitudes, values, and opinions

> Example: As part of an investigation into voting behaviour you interview a small number of 'floating voters' to try and discover what influences their voting.

- To collect information on sensitive issues

> Example: You are investigating changes in religious belief. You interview four young people about their attitudes to religion.

- You can interview adults in order to provide historical data – also known as **oral history**

> Example: You are studying changes in education. You conduct interviews with a parent and a grandparent about their experience of school. (This example is given in more detail on pages 88–89.)

- To collect information about the way of life of a particular group

> Example: As part of an investigation into youth culture you interview several members of a particular youth group about their lifestyle.

Step by step guide to doing in-depth interviews

1. Think of ways in-depth interviews might be effectively used in your research.

2. Decide who you would like to interview

- work out which kind of people you would like to interview and how many
- interviews are easily arranged if you already know the people you are interviewing
- if you wish to interview people you do not already know you must get in touch with them and ask permission for an interview, after explaining who you are, what you are doing, and how long the interview is likely to take.

3. Plan the interviews

- what are you trying to discover?
- how long will the interviews be?
- what topics do you wish to cover?
- what basic questions do you need to ask?
- how will you put the questions?
- how will you encourage the respondent to talk in detail?
- how will you collect the information?

Exercise 3

What do you think are the advantages and disadvantages of:–

a) Making notes on the interview as you go along?
b) Recording the interview?
c) Not taking notes and not recording the interview?

---

4. Arrange the interviews

- fix a convenient time for the respondent and yourself
- arrange a private place in which to conduct the interview
- you may wish to give your respondents a list of questions before the interview so that they can prepare answers
- if necessary, organise the loan of a cassette recorder. Make sure you know how to use it and that you have a blank cassette.

5. Do the interviews

- explain who you are, what you are investigating, and why you want to interview that person
- try to establish a friendly atmosphere in which the respondent will feel relaxed enough to discuss his or her views in depth; but don't get so friendly that the interview goes right off the point!

- don't make your note taking or the recorder and microphone too obvious – try and make the interview appear like a conversation
- be prepared for the interview to take a slightly different direction to the one you expected – don't go right off the point but have a flexible approach
- be prepared to think of some new questions and alter others in the light of what the respondent says
- if the respondent says less than you had hoped about a particular topic then you can 'prompt' them to say more in a variety of ways
- don't forget to thank the respondent when the interview is over.

Exercise 4

Suggest ways in which you could 'prompt' a respondent to talk in more detail about something.

Don't get so friendly that the interview goes right off the point!

6. Analyse and write up your findings

- it is important that you write up the interview as soon as possible after it has ended otherwise you will forget what happened. If you recorded the interview you must still write up the results
- the interview will probably be too long to write out in full so you will have to select parts which are of particular importance to your research
- you may wish to use headings and put the respondent's quotes under these, possibly with your own commentary alongside (see pp. 76–77)
- include in your analysis of the interviews:-

    a) how and why you planned the interviews as you did
    b) how the interviews went, including any problems you had
    c) what you discovered and how it relates to the rest of your investigation
    d) how you would organise the interviews differently if you were to do them again.

What's doing an in-depth interview really like?

'I had no intention of doing an interview at the time but as I walked past two policemen one said "hello" and that gave me the confidence to approach them.'

'I first asked the married respondents to describe a typical day. This was to give me a picture of their lifestyle and to see how tasks in the home were divided up.'

'Most of the questions arose from the answer before. I could explain the question if the respondent was in difficulty.'

'I wanted to see the expression on their faces when they answered certain questions.'

'If I didn't know the person I was interviewing we would just sit there and not say anything.'

'It was difficult for her to remember so far back and I had to repeat the questions quite a few times as she was deaf.'

'I wrote down a few quotes and tried to remember the rest. When I got home I'd forgotten.'

'I planned to tape the interviews but found that the recorder made people uneasy.'

'The only thing that went wrong was that the lead came out of the cassette recorder and so I missed half the interview.'

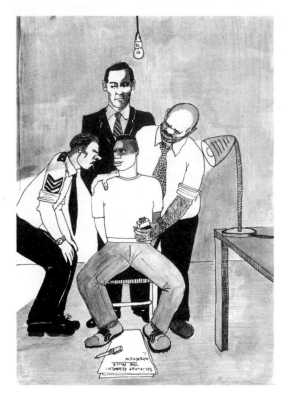

'As the policeman was used to interviewing people himself he would start asking me my views before he told me his. Sometimes I felt he was interviewing me.'

Doing in-depth interviews: reminders

Have you:-

- Thought how in-depth interviews could be used in your research?
- Planned and arranged the interviews thoroughly?
- Tried to create a relaxed atmosphere during the interviews, prompting the respondent where necessary?
- Written up the interview as soon as possible afterwards?
- Analysed and written about the interviews, including any problems you had doing them?

5 Observation

What is observation?

Observation involves looking and listening very carefully. We all watch other people sometimes, but we don't usually watch them in order to discover particular information about their behaviour. This is what observation in social science involves.

Observation can be of two types:-

Direct observation

The researcher observes without joining in in any way, thus people's behaviour should be unaffected by his or her presence. This kind of observation is similar to the way a bird watcher observes birds.

Participant observation

The researcher deliberately joins in with the activities of a group while observing them.

Why use observation?

● Observation allows the social scientist to study people in their 'natural setting' without their behaviour being influenced by the presence of a researcher.

● Observational data usually consists of detailed information about particular groups or situations. This kind of data can 'fill out' and provide a deeper, richer, understanding than survey work which tends to produce less detailed information about a larger number of people.

● A lot of what people do they 'take for granted': they do it 'naturally', they aren't aware of it. For example, studies have shown that teachers tend to pay more attention to boys than to girls but most teachers are unaware of this. You might be able to discover such 'taken for granted' behaviour by observation.

- Some methods only allow for the study of one individual at a time. Observation enables the researcher to study groups of people together, that is, it allows for the study of **interaction** between the members of a group, as in the example on pp. 91–92.

- An interview, for instance, only shows a person's views at one time. Observation involves the study of groups or situations over time, thus revealing changes in them.

- Some groups of people, such as school truants, may not agree to cooperate with methods of research such as interviews. Sometimes observation is the only way of finding out about such groups.

Exercise 1

In what ways might data gained through observation be different from data gained from questionnaires in the following instances?

a) finding out about football supporters' behaviour at matches
b) finding out about husbands and wives sharing tasks in the home
c) finding out about pupils' attitudes to school
d) finding out about who are the most influential figures in a peer group
e) finding out the number of cigarettes a person smokes a day.

How can I use direct observation?

- Observation of particular social conditions

  Example: Your research concerns housing. You walk round a particular area noting down types and conditions of housing.

- Observation of people and places during a visit

  Example: You are interested in any links which may exist between attendance at pre-school playgroups and educational achievement. You visit a playgroup and observe the facilities and the activities of children and staff.

Exercise 2

How might your presence affect people's behaviour during visits to the following places?

a) a school
b) a factory
c) a playgroup

- Observation of people in situations where your presence will not affect their behaviour

32

Example 1: As part of research into leisure activities and age you observe from the balcony of a swimming pool at different times on different days, noting down the ages of the people in the pool, and what their reasons for being there appear to be.

Example 2: You are investigating relationships between different groups of pupils at your school. You observe in the school dining hall, looking for answers to questions such as:-
Do boys and girls sit together or separately? Do the members of different year groups mix? Do pupils from different streams or bands sit together? Do pupils move their positions from day to day or do they always sit in the same place?

Exercise 3

a) Make a list of groups or situations it would be possible to observe without affecting people's behaviour.
b) For each group or situation on your list, give an example of how the observation could 'go wrong', with you ending up influencing people's behaviour.

Why choose participant observation?

When observing you have to interpret what you see. This can be difficult, especially when you are in a situation which is strange to you. For example, how might an outsider see a scuffle or an exchange of insults in a school playground – as fun, a game, harmless letting off steam, youthful high spirits, bad behaviour, or as real hostility? Remember that when you observe situations you must understand what people's behaviour means to **them**. This is made easier if you are actually joining in with the people or situation you are observing. There are also some situations and groups which it is simply not possible to observe without joining in, such as a group of friends.

How can I use participant observation?

It is unlikely that you will have enough time to get accepted into a group of people you are completely unfamiliar with, so participant observation might be better used in a group or situation you already have some contact with.

Example 1: You are interested in attitudes to work. During your Saturday job you observe the attitudes and behaviour of workers while joining in with the work at the same time.

Example 2: You join in with the activities of a group of football supporters, some of whom you already know. You aim to collect information about their behaviour at matches and on the journeys to and from grounds, their values, and the extent to which their support for a team influences the rest of their lives.

Example 3: As part of an investigation into families today you do participant observation in your own and a friend's family. You compare their values, lifestyles, roles and behaviour.

There is a more detailed example of participant observation on pp. 91–92.

Exercise 4

a) What problems might arise during participant observation in each of the above examples?

b) What other groups and situations might be suitable for participant observation? Why?

PARTICIPANT OBSERVATION IS NOT ALWAYS EASY.

Step by step guide to doing observation

1. Carefully consider what kind of observation might be useful for your research.

- what groups or situations would be relevant?
- is it possible and practical to observe them?
- should you use direct or participant observation?
- what could you find out from the observation?

2. Make any arrangements necessary for the observation to take place.

- ask for permission well in advance if you want to arrange a visit
- plan on which day or days the observation will take place and how long it will last.

3. Plan the headings you will use for your notes on the observation.

- decide exactly what you are trying to find out and work out suitable headings to make notes under.

  ● You might choose to use general headings

    Example: You are visiting a playgroup as part of research into the influence of pre-school education on educational achievement. You use headings such as: 'Activities children involved in which are similar to school', 'Purely play activities', 'Roles adults are playing'.

  ● If you are observing a particular situation you can simply tick off what is happening each minute or so. In order to do this you need to choose headings which will cover every possible occurrence.

    Example: You are observing a family meal as part of research into family relationships. Every minute you note down what is happening under headings such as: 'Father talking', 'Mother talking', 'Daughter talking', 'Silence'.

Exercise 5

What do you think would be the most suitable headings for observation of the following?

a) a visit to a factory as part of research into work satisfaction
b) observation in a school lesson as part of research into teaching methods
c) a visit to a Magistrates court as part of research into gender and crime
d) observation of parents and their children as part of research into sex role socialisation.

---

4. If you are doing participant observation you will have to decide whether to:
   a) remain 'hidden' – not tell anyone that you are observing them
   b) be 'open' – tell people that you are observing them.

Exercise 6

What do you think are the advantages and disadvantages of being:-

a) a 'hidden' participant observer?
b) an 'open' participant observer?
c) being 'open' with only one or two members of a group you are observing?

---

5. Do the observation

   – make sure you are properly prepared with paper, pen, and a clear idea of what you are looking for
   – make sure you make the notes as the observation is occurring or, if this is not possible, immediately afterwards – you don't want to forget what happened!
   – look and listen very carefully
   – remember to try not to influence the behaviour of the people you are observing, so be careful how you take notes.

6. Analyse and write up the results of your observation

   – look through your notes and work out what you have discovered
   – write up your observation including:-

      a) how and why you planned the observation as you did
      b) how the observation went, including problems you had doing it
      c) what you discovered and how this relates to other aspects of your research
      d) how you would organise the observation differently if you were to do it again.

What's doing observation really like?

'I looked at the sex of people working in local garages. I found that the 12 mechanics were all men and the only woman employed worked in the shop, taking money.'

'I tried to observe a family meal but there was an enormous row and I was not allowed to write anything down about it.'

'The observation was definitely the best part of the project.'

'I observed that, in my class, most girls waited to be asked a question whereas the boys put their hands up straight after the question was asked.'

'I was doing observation with someone else and we would get bored and talk, missing things that were going on.'

'Because pupils knew I was observing them they "put on a show" and misbehaved. If I were to do it again I would go into the class and pretend to work.'

'It was impossible to do participant observation when studying drugs because I would not have been capable of writing anything down.'

Doing observation: reminders

Have you:-

- Thought how observation could be used in your research?
- Got permission to do the observation where necessary?
- Planned out the headings you will use while taking notes?
- Made notes while you were doing the observation or straight afterwards?
- Tried not to influence the behaviour of anyone you were observing in any way?
- Analysed and written up the observation, including describing any problems you had in doing the observation?

6 Experiments

Experiments aim to discover the effect of one thing on another. You will probably have conducted some yourself during science lessons at school as they are commonly used in 'natural sciences' such as Physics and Chemistry. They are, however, much less common in the social sciences. One reason for this is that experiments need to take place in a controlled environment like a laboratory, where factors such as temperature can be fixed and measured. The social world just cannot be controlled in the same way. Nevertheless, it is possible to conduct certain kinds of social scientific experiments.

Warning: If you intend to conduct an experiment as part of your coursework you must discuss it with your teacher first as some experiments can cause people to get upset or offended.

How can I use experiments?

- To discover the unwritten rules which govern behaviour. These can be revealed by breaking the rules and watching other people's reactions.

   Example: You want to discover how people react when their 'personal space' is invaded. You walk down a street alongside, and at the same pace as, another person, although not communicating with them in any way. You watch their reaction to this: do they carry on walking regardless, or do they try to 'lose' you by speeding up, slowing down, or pausing to look in a shop window? You repeat the experiment several times in exactly the same way, noting down people's reactions afterwards.

- To discover the effect of groups on people's behaviour

   Example: You want to find out whether people are more likely to take risks when they are part of a group than when they are on their own. You give a number of individuals an imaginary story such as this: 'You are the captain of a sports team and are picking the team for a vitally important game. You have one player who can be brilliant but who is very unpredictable and who has been in and out of the team all year. Recently they have been playing badly. Do you include him or her in the team?' Your sample then has to make a decision and you count up their choices. You then give the same story to groups of people to discuss together and then reach a decision. You note down their decisions and compare the two sets of results: were the people in groups more likely to take the risk of including the unpredictable player in the team?

- To discover how the members of different social groups are treated

    Example: You are trying to discover how gender affects people's behaviour. In a busy shopping area you ask members of the public for directions to a particular place. At the same time in the same place the next week you get a person of similar age to yourself but of the opposite sex to ask for the same directions in the same way. You can then compare reactions: were people more or less helpful to the different sexes?

- To compare the behaviour of people from different social groups

    Example: As part of your research you are doing a questionnaire. You interview people outside a local Tesco's super-market and outside a high class department store. The shoppers at Tesco's are likely to be mostly working class and the department store shoppers middle class. As well as getting results from your questionnaire you will have conducted an experiment because you will be able to compare the reactions to being asked to fill in a questionnaire: which of the groups of people were more polite, helpful and cooperative?

Exercise 1

Design experiments to find out about the following. What problems might arise in conducting the experiments?

a) The effect of dress on people's behaviour.
b) How people react to members of different ethnic groups.
c) Whether men and women react differently in the same situation.

Step by step guide to doing an experiment

1. Think about the possibility of doing experiments in your research. Discuss possible experiments with your teacher, checking that they are possible to do, will prove useful, and will not cause offence.

2. Plan and prepare your experiment:-

    – make sure that any assistants know exactly what they are supposed to be doing
    – make sure you have all the equipment you need such as pens and paper.

3. Conduct the experiment – this may take place over several weeks in some cases. Remember that each part of the experiment must occur under the same conditions, at the same place and at the same time.

4. Make notes on your results
    – what do they show?
    – how could your experiment have been improved?
    – what mistakes did you make?

What's it really like to do an experiment?

'My teacher wouldn't let me do any of the experiments I wanted to.'

'I left a 10p piece on the pavement and waited to see how people would react and who would pick it up. The first person who passed picked it up. That was the end of the experiment.'

'I did an experiment in which I smiled all through my lessons at school in order to see people's reactions. A teacher told me I was being rude and put me in detention. I learnt a lot from that experiment.'

Doing experiments: reminders

Have you:

- Thought what experiments you could use?
- Discussed them with your teacher?
- Made sure that each part of the experiment took place under the same conditions?
- Made notes on your results including any mistakes you made?

Secondary Sources

You don't have to collect data yourself. A vast range of material is already available, ranging from government statistics to children's comics.

Material you 'borrow' is called **secondary data**. It can be very useful but you should remember that:-

- It may not be **reliable**: you will often not know how accurate it is. Of course some kinds of secondary data are likely to be more reliable than others; government figures are likely to be more trustworthy than an article in *The Sun*, for instance.

- It may be **biased**: favouring one point of view. You should analyse material for bias, possibly using **content analysis** (see page 53).

- It is not a good idea to copy out large amounts of secondary data.

- Secondary data should always be commented on: why it is included, how it might be unreliable or biased, and so on.

- Secondary data should always be used in a way which **adds something** to your research.

The following four sections deal with methods of collecting and using secondary data.

7 Official Statistics

What are official statistics?

Official statistics are data in numerical form produced by local and national government bodies. Every branch of government needs information about social and economic developments relevant to its work. A wide range of facts and figures are needed in order to plan policies for the future.

Exercise 1

Why might a government need to know:

a) How many people own cars?
b) How many babies are being born?
c) The ethnic origins of the population?
d) Whether houses possess basic amenities?

Every ten years the government carries out a **census** of the British population and has done so since 1871. This involves every household in Britain filling in a questionnaire which provides information concerning population, families, housing, work, transport and education.

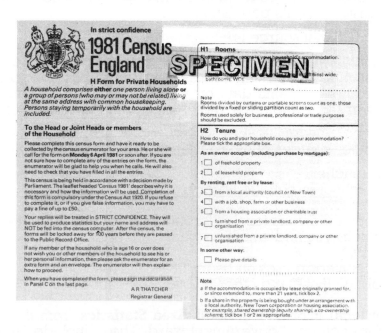

The most recent census was in 1981.

Where can I get official statistics from?

The following books, published each year, contain a selection of the most interesting official statistics.

Social Trends This consists of a wide range of statistics, many of them relating to changes over time. There is also some discussion of them.

Annual Abstract of Statistics Similar to **Social Trends** but more detailed statistics without any discussion.

Key Data Contains the most important social and economic statistics in any year.

Regional Trends This presents a range of statistics on the various regions of the UK. It includes data on topics such as law, employment, health and housing.

World Statistics in Brief This contains the basic facts about population, trade, tourism, health and education for every country.

Britain: An Official Handbook Some of the information in this book is not in a statistical form but it does contain a large amount of basic information about the economic, political and social affairs of Britain and its population.

A useful semi-official source is:-

British Social Attitudes The statistics in this book concern people's attitudes to various issues of current public concern. The 1986 edition contains data on attitudes to work, pollution, nuclear war, education, the welfare state and a variety of social and moral issues.

These and other sources of official statistics, may be available from:

- your teacher
- your school or college library.

If they are not, then your local reference library will have them. Ask the librarian to help you find what you want.

The list of useful addresses on pages 96–101 gives you further information on how to obtain these and other official publications.

If you want **local** information **Small Area Statistics** from the census are available for each local government ward. These include information on the age, sex, marital status, country of birth and economic activity of the people in your immediate locality. These are also available from reference libraries.

You can also write to the relevant department of your local authority for information.

How can I use official statistics?

There are such a variety of official statistics available that you will probably find some which are useful, even if they are not exactly about the issue you are researching.

Once you have found some relevant figures it is not a good idea to simply include them and hope that they 'speak for themselves'. In order to avoid this you should:-

1. Make sure you fully understand the statistics

The following table from **Social Trends** concerns the changing composition of households from 1961–1981.

Check the area covered by the table

Look at the years covered by the table

Look at the title of the table → **Households: by type**

Great Britain   Percentages and thousands

Make sure you know what the figures represent

Is the table divided into sub-headings?

	Percentages						Thousands		
	1961	1971	1976	1981	1982	1983	1961	1971	1981
No family									
One person									
Under retirement age	4	6	6	8	8	8	726	1,122	1,469
Over retirement age	7	12	15	14	15	16	1,193	2,198	2,771
Two or more people									
One or more over retirement age	3	2	2	2	1	1	536	444	387
One family									
Married couple only	26	27	27	26	27	27	4,147	4,890	4,989
Married couple with 1 or 2 dependent children	30	26	26	25	24	24	4,835	4,723	4,850
Married couple with 3 or more dependent children	8	9	8	6	6	6	1,282	1,582	1,100
Married couple with independent child(ren) only	10	8	7	8	8	8	1,673	1,565	1,586
Lone parent with at least 1 dependent child	2	3	4	5	4	5	367	515	916
Lone parent with independent child(ren) only	4	4	4	4	4	4	721	712	720
Two or more families	3	1	1	1	1	1	439	263	170
Total households	100	100	100	100	100	100	16,189	18,317	19,493

Total sample size

45

Exercise 2

What trends does the table on page 45 show:-

a) In the number of single parent families?
b) In the numbers of people living on their own?
c) In the number of nuclear families (married couples with children)?

2. Interpret the figures: work out exactly what they mean

Unemployed school leavers

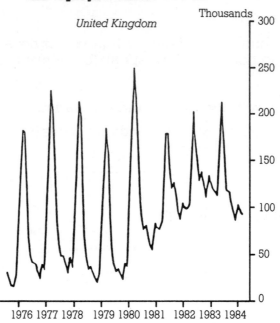

United Kingdom

Source: *Department of Employment.*

Exercise 3

a) Why do the figures increase dramatically about three-quarters of the way through each year?
b) What is the underlying trend of the figures?

3. Use the statistics in a way which adds something to your research

You might use official statistics to:-

● Provide background information for use in an introduction

Example: Your research concerns working class underachievement in education. You include statistics showing the

46

growth in the number of places in higher education since the Second World War. This can be the basis for a discussion about increasing opportunities for all classes.

- Compare your findings to official figures

  Example: You find that a majority of your female sample go out to work. You use official statistics to see whether your findings are similar to the national picture. If they are not, you can discuss reasons why this might be the case.

- Give a national picture when your research is confined to a local area

  Example: You have conducted a questionnaire on housing conditions in your locality. You include statistics on national housing conditions and compare them, discussing possible reasons for the differences.

- Compare different areas

  Example: Your research concerns unemployment. You include statistics showing the varying levels of unemployment in different regions and discuss how and why this is the case.

- Give a picture of change over time

  Example: You are researching into family size among different classes. You use figures from the 1891, 1921, 1951 and 1981 Censuses to show how average family size is changing.

- To show whether people's attitudes reflect official statistics

  Example: Your research is on the subject of racism. In your questionnaire to white people you include a question asking respondents how many black people they think are resident in the UK. You compare people's guesses to the official figures and discuss why they are different.

Exercise 4

What official figures might you look for, and how would you use them, if you were investigating the following hypotheses?

a) British society is becoming less religious.
b) Poverty no longer exists.
c) Women have achieved equality.
d) The British education system offers equal opportunities to all.

Can I always trust Official Statistics?

Official Statistics are collected very carefully using very large samples – the census covers **every** household in Britain – and for this reason, as well as their easy availability, they are often used as data by social scientists. However, this does not mean you should accept them at face value. You should carefully consider the ways in which the statistics may be unreliable, or at least need careful interpretation.

Some official figures are very unreliable, especially when compared over time. One example is criminal statistics. These are collected by the police and are often used by the media to claim, for instance, that the crime rate is rapidly rising.

Daily Mail

FRIDAY, MAY 23, 1986   20p

CRIME RATE SOARS AGAIN

By PETER BURDEN, Chief Crime Reporter

FRIGHTENING new crime figures revealed today put the Government's law and order policies under increased pressure.

In a week when attention has been focused on the Police Federation conference—and the delegates' complaints of serious undermanning — the figures make disturbing reading.

Muggings, violence against the person, sex crimes and robberies in the Metropolitan Police area all rose sharply in the first quarter of this year.

The Scotland Yard figures are generally regarded as a barometer of what is happening in the rest of the country.

Source: *Daily Mail,* May 23, 1986.

48

This may not necessarily be the case. There may be other reasons why it **appears** that the crime rate is rising.

Exercise 5

How might criminal statistics be affected by:-

a) The police computerising their records?
b) The ownership of telephones increasing?
c) The police in one area 'clamping down' on pornography?
d) Supermarkets beginning to replace smaller shops?

Another case where official figures may be considered unreliable is unemployment. Groups like the TUC (Trades Union Congress) argue that the government seriously underestimates the real amount of unemployment and sometimes changes the way in which the figures are calculated in order to make unemployment appear less. In fact it is unclear which groups should and should not appear in the unemployment figures.

Exercise 6

What arguments can you think of for and against these groups being included in the unemployment figures?

a) Young people on Youth Training Schemes.
b) Claimants who are not really looking for work.
c) 'Job changers' who are out of work for four weeks or less.
d) Married women at home.

When you use official statistics you should think carefully about the ways the figures might not be reliable and discuss these in your research.

You should also remember to acknowledge the source of the figures you use.

What's using Official Statistics really like?

'The problem with the official graph was that it didn't show all the information I wanted.'

'Using official statistics was useful because they gave a national picture, and covered the whole population. It would have been impossible for me to collect that information.'

'The results of my questionnaire were quite similar to the official figures.

'I copied some figures into my project but I don't really know why because I couldn't understand them.'

'I compared my results to the official youth unemployment figures and found that youth unemployment is much less where I live than it is in the country as a whole.'

'I couldn't find any figures on how many MPs were gay.'

Using Official Statistics: reminders

Have you:-

- Found those most relevant to your research?
- Made sure you understand them fully?
- Discussed what they show?
- Used them in a way that adds to your research?
- Acknowledged their source?
- Discussed ways in which they might be unreliable?

8 The Mass Media

What are the mass media?

The mass media are ways of communicating with a very large number of people. They include:-

- television
- radio
- newspapers
- magazines and comics
- advertisements
- films and videos

Where do I get mass media material from?

Always keep a look out for articles and programmes relevant to your research. You may not actually have to buy newspapers and magazines.

- Ask friends and relations if they buy newspapers, magazines or comics you want to use. They will probably give them to you when they have finished reading them.
- Your library should contain copies of daily newspapers and some magazines.
- If you wish to study the contents of radio or TV programmes you will need a recording of them. If you do not have suitable recording equipment, your school may be able to record them for you.

How can I use the mass media?

Items such as articles, news stories and adverts can be used simply to add to, or illustrate, points you are making. The media can also provide you with visual material which may enhance the presentation of your research.

If you use the media in these ways you must remember to:

- Not copy large amounts out.
- Add your own comments explaining why you are including the material.
- Make sure the material is used in a way which adds something to your research.

However, there may be a more important way in which you can use the mass media in your coursework:-

Content Analysis

The mass media play an important part in influencing public opinion. If your research topic appears in the media you can analyse the way which it is dealt with (or ignored) and discover how the public's attitudes may be influenced.

Journalists do not simply report 'facts'. They try and make their article or programme exciting and interesting to their audience. You need to study how material may be distorted and whether the journalists, or their bosses, or somebody else's point of view is being put across.

Exercise 1

a) In this example, are the TV and newspaper reporting 'facts' about the demonstration?
b) In what way, if any, is the media's coverage of the demonstration misleading?
c) How have the media managed to give the impression of the demonstration that they do?
d) Using this example, do 'facts speak for themselves'?

Content analysis is one method social scientists use to analyse the products of the mass media and other secondary data. One way of using content analysis is to count up the number of times certain words, ideas, pictures or images appear in the media. A content analysis frame is often needed and a simple example of one is included in Exercise 2. Every content analysis frame is different according to what is being investigated. You will find a detailed example of content analysis on pp. 92–93.

There are a variety of ways in which content analysis might be used in your research:-

- To try to detect bias or distortion in the mass media

  Example: You are investigating football hooliganism. You use the article below to make various points about the media's coverage of the subject.

Exercise 2

Fans in knives battle

SIX fans were injured in bloody clashes at a London soccer match last night.

At one stage the game between West Ham and Chelsea was held up as rival fans fought it out with knives and bottles.

Three of the injured needed hospital treatment after the battles at West Ham's Upton Park ground. There were no arrests.

Words suggesting 'violence' used in article	
'Facts' included in article	

a) Copy out this content analysis frame and fill it in.
b) What impression of the football match do you think the writer of the article is trying to put across?
c) What evidence is there in the article that the football match may not have been as violent as it suggests?

- To discover how different media treat the same issue.

  Example: Your research is about the public's attitude to CND. You compare TV, radio and newspapers reporting of a large CND demonstration using headings such as; estimated size of crowd, amount of space/time given to story, where did story appear, who was quoted?

- To compare news coverage in the different media

  Example: You tape local and national radio and TV news bulletins on one evening. You also obtain copies of the newspapers the next day. You compare the emphasis different news items are given and the way they are presented in the various media, concentrating on issues such as the language used to describe people and events.

Exercise 3

The mass media often use words and phrases similar to those on the wall above to describe the kind of people in the cartoon.
a) Which of these words or phrases give a favourable view of the 'fighters' and which unfavourable?
b) What might influence the media in their choice of words to describe the different kinds of 'fighters'?

- To compare the media's emphasis on an issue with an official view

Example: You count up the kinds of crimes which are covered in newspapers and TV news broadcasts. You also watch as many TV crime series as you can in a week, counting up which crimes they deal with. You then compare your results with the official statistics of the number of different offences committed.

- To compare the media's treatment of a topic with your own research

    Example: You are investigating the leisure interests of girls. You count up the amount of space given to different leisure activities in a sample of girls magazines and compare this with the results of a questionnaire on leisure you have already given to a sample of girls.

- To compare the 'conventional' and 'alternative' media

    Example: You compare the portrayal of the Conservative Party in *The Daily Telegraph* and *The Morning Star* over a week.

- To discover how particular groups of people are presented in the media: what images and **stereotypes** the media use

    Example: Your research concerns women's participation in sport. You count up how many photographs of each sex occur in a selection of sporting magazines.

Exercise 4

a) Families in adverts and cartoons often appear rather like this one. What does this tell us about the stereotypical view of the family?
b) Look at the figures for the composition of households on p. 45. What do these tell us about the accuracy of the stereotypical view of the family?

- Content Analysis can also be used to study other media such as books.

  Example: See pp. 92–93.

Exercise 5

How might content analysis be used in a research project on the following topics?

a) racism
b) young people and drug abuse
c) roles in the family
d) cigarette smoking

What's using the mass media really like?

'I looked at each daily newspaper's coverage of the Budget. I studied headlines – they give an indication of what the newspaper thinks is important; the editorials – these are openly biased; and cartoons – which are supposed to be funny but also show the paper's views.'

'Buying all the magazines was really expensive.'

'My content analysis showed me that reporters put things in their stories just to make them more exciting.'

'I recorded every TV soap opera in one week – I used up four video tapes.'

'I videoed all the news programmes on one night but my dad taped "The Benny Hill Show" over them.'

Using the mass media: reminders

Have you:-

- Collected relevant material from the mass media?
- Thought carefully about the most useful ways to use the media in your research?
- Worked out the most appropriate content analysis frame and completed it?
- Analysed your results?
- Kept a note of the media material you've used, including their dates?

9 Books

It is unlikely that you are the first person to research and write about a particular topic. Whatever you are investigating there are probably books in your school and local library which you will find useful. Ask your teacher for advice.

Certain kinds of books might prove particularly helpful:-

1. Other social research in the same area
2. Books containing relevant historical material
3. Books containing relevant comparative material (information about different societies)
4. Novels
5. Reference books

1. How can I use other social research?

Other social scientists are likely to have already collected data on the area of social life you're investigating. You should certainly look at their work but beware! Some books by social scientists are very difficult to understand. For this reason you might prefer to look for summaries of their work in textbooks that your teacher or library may have.

- Before you start your research, books can help by showing you:-

    - the aspects of your area of study that other social researchers have focused on
    - the methods which have been used to study similar topics
    - the **concepts** (words or phrases developed to aid the understanding of something) other researchers have used. You may wish to use these in your research.

- It can act as a basis for discussion of other researchers' methods and conclusions.

- It can be used in a conclusion to compare to your own results. You can discuss how and why yours are similar or different.

Exercise 1

Your research is concerned with young people's choice of careers. Here is an extract from research into schoolboys in the north east by Paul Corrigan. In what ways could you use this material in your research? You might think about:

- how representative the data is
- its use in comparing regions and social classes
- at what point in your research you might use it and how.

What do you expect *to be doing when you leave school?*	Professional	8
	Skilled	24
	Unskilled	29
	Services	17
	No answer	15

It is not easy to compare this data with other studies since my interest was self-consciously concerned with working-class boys and their 'careers'. There are, however, a much larger number of boys entering the services (other studies have suggested only 2 per cent) and a smaller number expecting to enter skilled manual work. Both of these characteristics are explicable in terms of the local working-class community culture. The recruitment for the Army and Navy represents an important tradition in an area racked by prolonged structural unemployment. This is reinforced by two factors. Firstly, the boys expected that it would be difficult for them to get a job (48 per cent thought this) and in this atmosphere going into the Army is one of the safer bets for single men. Secondly, when I moved to the north-east, I was immediately struck by the amount of recruiting done by the services every July and August. All the big towns in the area have large numbers of tanks, field guns, and so forth in strategic places at this time of the year.

Source: *Schooling the Smash Street Kids* by Paul Corrigan, Macmillan, Basingstoke, 1979, p. 77.

2. How can I use historical material?

Every part of society changes over time, including the part you are investigating. Your research should take this into account by using historical material. This can be in the form of oral history (see pp. 26 and 88–89). There may also be a local history group in your area which could help you.

Exercise 2

Your research is about the extent of street crime. How could you use this 'joke' advertisement from Punch magazine in 1862?

(ADVERTISEMENT)

DO YOU WANT TO AVOID BEING STRANGLED!!

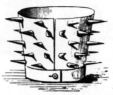

If so, try our Patent Antigarotte collar, which enables Gentlemen to walk the streets of London in perfect safety at all hours of the day or night.

THESE UNIQUE ARTICLES OF DRESS

Are made to measure, of the hardest steel, and are warranted to withstand the grip of

THE MOST MUSCULAR RUFFIAN IN THE METROPOLIS,

Who would get black in the face himself before he could make the slightest impression upon his intended victim. They are highly polished, and

Elegantly Studded with the Sharpest Spikes,

Thus combining a most *recherché* appearance with perfect protection from the murderous attacks which occur every day in the most frequented thoroughfares. Price 7s. 6d, or six for 40s.

WHITE, CHOKER, AND Co.

EFFECT OF THE ANTIGAROTTE COLLAR ON A GARROTTER

Source: *Hooligan* by Geoffrey Pearson, Macmillan, Basingstoke, 1985, p. 139.

3. How can I use comparative material?

Comparisons between different societies have always been a popular method of social research.

● Comparing 'social problems' and different approaches to their causes and solutions can give fresh insights into the way we deal with them.

WHO WOULD YOU SAY WAS 'NORMAL'?

Exercise 3

This is an extract from a study by Margaret Mead of the Tchambuli tribe who live in New Guinea. If your research was about sex roles in Britain how could you use this material?

> The women go with shaven heads, unadorned, determinedly busy about their affairs. The men wear lovely ornaments, they do the shopping, they carve and paint and dance. Men whose hair is long enough wear curls, and the others make false curls out of rattan rings.

Source: *Male and Female* by Margaret Mead, Penguin, Harmondsworth, 1962, pp. 106–7.

---

4. How can I use novels?

● Although novels are not 'facts' they can be used to put across particular ideas or the atmosphere of a time, place, group, or situation. You might want to copy a small passage from the book or write your own account of the book, emphasising why it is relevant to your coursework.

Example: You are investigating communism. You write an account of *Animal Farm* by George Orwell, including some quotes from it, as well as an explanation of why Orwell wrote the book. This will show many of the faults people find with present day communist societies.

● You might want to use children's books. These are particularly useful for content analysis (see pp. 92–93).

Exercise 4

You are investigating racism. You decide to include this extract from *The Story of Dr. Dolittle* by Hugh Lofting in your research project. What could you write about it?

Well, that night Prince Bumpo came secretly to the Doctor in prison and said to him: 'White Man, I am an unhappy prince. Years ago I went in search of the Sleeping Beauty, whom I had read of in a book. And having travelled through the world many days, I at last found her and kissed the lady very gently to awaken her – as the book said I should. 'Tis true indeed that she awoke. But when she saw my face she cried out, "Oh, he's black!" And she ran away and wouldn't marry me – but went to sleep again somewhere else. So I came back, full of sadness, to my father's kingdom. Now I hear that you are a wonderful magician and have many powerful potions. So I come to you for help. If you will turn me white, so that I may go back to the Sleeping Beauty, I will give you half my kingdom and anything besides you ask.'

'Prince Bumpo,' said the Doctor, looking thoughtfully at the bottles in his medicine-bag, 'supposing I made your hair a nice blonde colour – would not that do instead to make you happy?'

'No', said Bumpo. 'Nothing else will satisfy me. I must be a white prince.'

Source: *The Story of Dr. Dolittle* by Hugh Lofting, Jonathan Cape, London, 1922, pp. 134–5.

---

5. How can I use reference books?

Your school and local libraries should have a large number of reference books such as encyclopaedias which might contain information useful to your coursework. Ask your teacher to suggest what reference books may be helpful.

Example 1: You are investigating whether Britain is becoming 'two nations' with a widening gap between living standards in the relatively well off south east and those in other regions. As part of your research you look at a copy of *Who's Who*, a book which lists most 'top' people in business, politics, the military and entertainment. You take a random sample of entries and see which part of the country they live in.

Example 2: Your hypothesis is that independent businesses are dying out in your town. You jot down the names of all the shops in the town centre. You then look up the names of the owners in *Who Owns Whom*, the directory of company ownership, which is probably available in your local reference library. This will show you what proportion of the shops are owned by large companies and which are independent.

(adapted from 'Who Owns Whom' by Pat McNeill, in *Handbook for Sociology Teachers* edited by Gomm and McNeill, Heinemann, London, 1982, pp. 163–5).

What's using books really like?

'Other sociologist's work put things into perspective and made my views clearer.'

'I actually went to the library, but I couldn't find any books on the National Front.'

'I looked through some textbooks before I started my project to see what other people had discovered.'

'I tried to read some books but couldn't understand them.'

'My history teacher lent me some very useful books.'

'I think my project is much more interesting than anything I've read by anyone else.'

Using other books: reminders

Have you:-

- Asked for advice about, and looked for, the most useful books for your research, particularly:-
    - Related social research
    - Historical material
    - Comparative material
    - Novels
    - Reference books?

- Used this material at the most suitable points in your research?
- Used this material in a way which adds something to your research?
- Kept a list of the books you've used?

10 Pressure groups and other organisations

Many organisations exist to put forward particular points of view, or to represent the interests of various groups in the community. Organisations that try to influence decision making are called **pressure groups**.

Examples

- Some are paid for by public donations — Amnesty International, RSPCA

- Some are paid for by the people whose interests they represent — Trades Union Congress, Confederation of British Industry

- Some are paid for by local or central government grants — Equal Opportunities Commission, Commission for Racial Equality

Most of these organisations produce publicity material and information. This is usually available to the public, often free of charge.

Are there any pressure groups relevant to my research?

There are so many pressure groups that it is likely that one or more exist which will be able to provide you with useful information. You will find a list of names and addresses on pages 96–101. However, the organisations on this list are only a small proportion of the enormous number of pressure groups that exist. The list does not include, for instance, local pressure groups which may be campaigning in your area on issues such as road building or pollution.

How can I get information from pressure groups?

Most organisations will send you material if you write to them enclosing a large stamped addressed envelope.

Here is an example of the kind of letter you might send:-

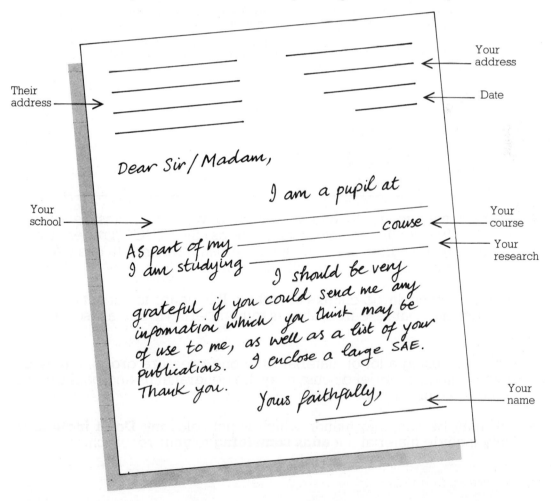

Their address →

Your address ←

Date ←

Your school →

Your course ←

Your research ←

Dear Sir / Madam,

I am a pupil at _____ course

As part of my _____
I am studying _____ I should be very grateful if you could send me any information which you think may be of use to me, as well as a list of your publications. I enclose a large SAE.
Thank you.

Yours faithfully,

Your name ←

How can I use the information they send me?

- It is important to remember that the material you are sent will represent the point of view of the organisation: it will be **biased** in favour of their views. For this reason you should discuss their material **critically**, not simply include it without comment.

Exercise 1

In what ways might some people disagree with the views of 'Life'?

Save the Unborn Child

LIFE is a voluntary non-denominational and non-party-political association of people who are opposed to all direct abortion because,

since human life begins at conception, i.e. fertilisation, and since all human life should be equally protected by the law from conception to natural death whether or not the human being concerned is wanted or handicapped,

it follows that:

1. Deliberate and direct destruction of unborn human life is always wrong.

2. The unborn child should enjoy the full protection of the law.

3. The positive alternative to abortion should be made available to women with problem pregnancies.

- Another way to try to avoid bias is to write to pressure groups representing different interests such as the TUC (Trades Union Congress) and CBI (Confederation of British Industry). In this way you will be able to assess alternative viewpoints.

- Never copy out large chunks of writing. It is better to cut out and stick material into your research, always remembering to add a discussion of it.

- If you are using a lot of material from one pressure group, it may be worth including a brief discussion of the general aims and background of the pressure group.

- You may be sent information which is not relevant. **Don't include it**. Only include material if it **adds something** to your research.

- You can use pressure group material such as photographs, diagrams and cartoons to improve the presentation of your coursework.

LINKS 23

Quarterly Magazine Of
Third World First

THE COLONIAL CARVE-UP

What's using material from pressure groups and other organisations really like?

'I wrote to all the major political parties and compared the material they sent me.'

'I couldn't think of any group or organisation to write to.'

'Even though I put stamped addressed envelopes in with every questionnaire I sent to different embassies, I received very few back.'

'I got replies from most of the employers I wrote to about their YTS schemes.'

'I received a lot of brochures with very useful photographs in; they made my project look much better.'

'I wrote to the Army for information and a recruitment officer called round, much to my surprise!'

Pressure groups and other organisations: reminders

Have you:-

- Written to all pressure groups and organisations which might help you?
- Discussed possible bias in the material you've used?
- Avoided copying out large amounts?
- Commented on the material you've included?
- Used visual material to improve the presentation of your research?
- Used the material in a way which adds something to your research?

11 Choosing research methods

Your course may involve two or three pieces of coursework, or it may require one long piece of research where you are encouraged to use a variety of methods. Either way, you will have to decide which of the methods of data collection described in the last section of the book are most useful to you. Choosing methods carefully is important because unsuitable methods will seriously affect the quality of your results and make your coursework harder. Also, the examiner will be looking for the reasons why you chose the methods you did.

How should I choose which methods to use?

The previous sections of the book explained the sources of data available to you. No one method of collecting data is better than any other; the method or methods you choose depend mostly on two things:-

a) What groups of people you want to obtain information about.
b) What exactly you want to find out about those groups.

Let's look at these points in turn.

a) It is impossible, or at least very difficult, to use some methods with some groups. This might be because:-

- Members of some groups may be unwilling to cooperate with questionnaires or interviews.
- It is impossible or impractical to observe some groups and situations.
- There may be no secondary data available.
- It may be impossible to contact some groups so no primary data collection is possible at all.

Exercise 1

For each of the four points above choose two groups or situations which could be examples of each and explain which methods of data collection **could** be used to study them.

---

b) Different methods of data collection produce different kinds of data.

Think carefully about the information you want:-

- Is it already available as secondary data?

    - in official statistics
    - in the reports of government and other organisations
    - in reference books
    - in other sociologists' work
    - in the mass media
    - in history books

- Do you want to analyse this data, possibly using content analysis?

If the information you want is not already available in the form you want, or you don't think it's reliable, or you want to produce your own results to compare to it, then you will want to collect your own data: primary data.

What kind of primary data do you want?

- Do you want quite straightforward information from a large sample which you can express in statistics? This is known as **quantitative data** and can be collected by:-

questionnaires:	These can cover a large sample but questions must be kept simple and response rate can be low.
structured interviews:	In this case the questionnaire is read out. The presence of an interviewer means that questions can be explained and the response rate is likely to be higher than that for a questionnaire.
observation:	As long as it is possible to observe a particular place, group or situation, you can count or add up the number of times certain things occur.

- Do you want information which is mostly about attitudes, opinions, values and lifestyles in more detail from a smaller sample which you will probably not be able to express in a statistical form? This is known as **qualitative data** and can be collected using:-

in-depth interviews:	You establish a friendly relationship with the respondent and have a detailed 'chat' about whatever interests you as a researcher.
participant observation:	If it is possible for you to actually join in with a particular group then you can gain valuable insights into what makes the group 'tick'.

All these methods of data collection are discussed in detail in the previous sections and you should make your choice of methods after reading that part of the book. Often you will find it useful to use two or more methods within a single research project.

PARTICIPANT OBSERVATION MEANS JOINING IN!

Why use more than one method?

● One method might lead on to another as shown in the following chart.

> observation → interviews
> observation → questionnaires
> interviews → observation
> interviews → questionnaires
> questionnaires → observation
> questionnaires → interviews

Example: You are studying youth unemployment. You begin by conducting participant observation among a group of young unemployed people. This provides you with information on what is important in their lives, what worries and concerns them, and how they see their situation. With this information you are in a better position to ask sensible, meaningful and relevant questions in a questionnaire or interview.

71

Exercise 1

You are investigating how people spend their retirement years. You construct a questionnaire but find you are asking the wrong questions and obtaining little useful information. This is simply because you have little knowledge on which to base your questionnaire.

What methods might be more suitable for your research? Give reasons for your answer.

Exercise 2

You begin by interviewing people about why they have chosen certain names for their children. You think you have found a connection between social class and choice of names but need a much larger sample to test this hypothesis. Interviews take too long.

Which method might be more suitable? Give reasons for your answer.

- If your coursework consists of one longer research project then using a mixture of research methods to give you a variety of data should produce a balanced account of the topic you are investigating. It will show the examiner that you are capable of using different methods to give you a fuller picture.

You might use a mixture of:–

- – Primary and secondary data
- – Quantitative and qualitative data

Exercise 3

Choose suitable methods for investigating the following hypotheses. Give reasons for your choice in each case.

a) Traditional sex roles are disappearing.
b) YTS is just an excuse for cheap labour.
c) Voters have little knowledge of politics today.
d) Education has not really changed since 1945.
e) Males dominate most sporting and leisure activities.

Case study

A case study involves the detailed investigation of a single example of whatever you're interested in; for instance a study of one group of people or of one place such as a factory. You will not be able to claim that your results are representative, but will instead concentrate on a close understanding of that particular example. A variety of methods can be used in a case study. You might choose to study, for instance, one group of friends, one club, or one family. Look at the examples of case studies of a super-market and a pop group on pp. 89–92.

Exercise 4

You are doing a case study of a large department store where you have a Saturday job and also work during the holidays.

Consider the different methods you could use in doing a case study of the department store.

What's choosing methods really like?

'I used a variety of methods because I wanted a variety of information.'

'Many of the facts I discovered doing my questionnaire had to be backed up through in-depth interviews.'

'I used mostly observation because it seemed to be the most enjoyable method.'

'I chose to do some questionnaires but I think this was just because every-body else in the class was – I could have got the information I wanted from official statistics.'

'I couldn't do participant observation with the drugtakers because I would have been unable to write anything down.'

Choosing research methods: reminders

Have you:–

- Considered what you want to find out about whom?
- Thought which method or methods would be most suitable to discover this?
- Considered the possibility of a case study?
- Written about how and why you chose the methods you did?

12 Presenting Data

Once you have completed a particular piece of data collection you are faced with the problem of how you intend to present your findings. Marks will be given to you for clear and accurate presentation of data so this is an important aspect of your research project.

How should I present quantitative data?

You have a number of choices to make in presenting your statistical data. Generally, the clearest methods involve the use of tables or graphs.

- **Tables**

    A table simply refers to the presentation of figures in columns and rows. The reader can see quickly what sort of data is being presented.

    Example: Table to show the number of times certain events occurred during a variety of seventy minute fourth year lessons.

	Maths	Physics	English	Geography	Total
Individual pupils told off	8	12	3	9	32
Whole class told off	5	8	5	3	21
Individual pupils praised	0	0	1	0	1
Whole class praised	0	0	0	0	0
Questions asked to individual pupils	0	5	1	0	6
Questions asked to whole class	7	4	9	0	20

(Neill Gardiner)

- **Bar Graphs**

    Bar graphs use columns to show how often certain things occur or particular answers are given.

    Example: Bar Graphs to show the number of times males and females are shown performing traditional and non-traditional sex roles in three young children's comics.

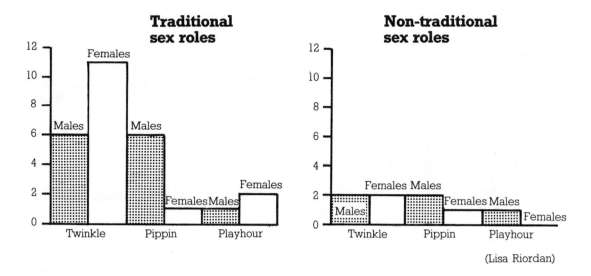

Traditional sex roles

Non-traditional sex roles

(Lisa Riordan)

● Pie Charts

Pie charts are circles which are divided up into 'slices' to show the different proportions which make up the whole. The larger the proportion, the larger the slice. In order to construct a pie chart you have to turn your data into percentages and then work out appropriate angles.

Example: Pie chart to show answers to the question: 'Which member or members of the family should be chiefly responsible for the housework?'

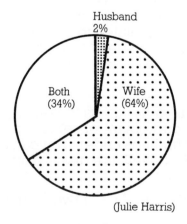

Husband 2%

Both (34%)

Wife (64%)

(Julie Harris)

75

When presenting quantitative data:-

- Describe how the data was collected, including any problems you had collecting it, especially if they may have affected the reliability of the data.

- Only turn your figures into percentages if you have a large sample (say, over 50).

- Label each graph or table carefully.

- For each table and graph you include, describe briefly what the figures show, and what conclusions you draw from them concerning the aims of your research.

How should I present qualitative data?

Qualitative data is not usually statistical but still needs to be presented clearly and in a way which is related to the aims of your research. Some of the data you collect during an in-depth interview or participant observation might not be relevant to your research and should not, therefore, be included.

- You may well have used headings to help you make notes on your in-depth interviews or participant observation. These headings can be used to present your findings under. You can use quotes and examples under such headings, as well as a description and analysis of what was said or observed.

   Example: (from observation of two cannabis smokers)

   ### Attitudes to each other

   When they were not taking drugs they tended to take matters very seriously and had more arguments. These

76

were normally started by the man. They did, however, seem to trust each other and share equal roles in house-work. When they took drugs things became less serious so when they started arguing one of them would say something silly and they would both end up laughing.

(Abigail Bridgeman)

Exercise 2

What headings might you use in presenting the results of the following research?

a) An in-depth interview with an old age pensioner about their education.
b) Participant observation at a youth club.

- Use quotes from in-depth interviews in order to highlight points you wish to make and to add colour and interest to the presentation of your coursework

> Example: (from an in-depth interview with a football supporter)
> 'I ended up with a broken nose and two black eyes but I made sure the other geezer was worse off ... I never go looking for trouble, but if it comes I never run away.'

When presenting qualitative data:-

- Describe how the research was carried out, including any problems you had doing it.

- Use headings to keep your presentation relevant.

- Use quotes and examples from your research.

- Analyse your results: how do they relate to your general aims or hypothesis?

How should I present secondary data?

As you have seen secondary data can come in a wide variety of forms, ranging from official statistics to cartoons. However, there are certain general points to bear in mind when presenting secondary data.

- Always put a note by the material explaining where it is taken from. An alternative is to give each piece of secondary data you include a number and list each number and the source it refers to at the end of the research project.

- It is perfectly acceptable to copy out, or stick in, small amounts from books and other sources as long as they add something to your research. Make sure you put this material in quotation marks so that the examiner can see that it is not your own writing.

- Always comment on the secondary data you include:–
    - why have you included it?
    - what does it show?
    - how reliable is it – does it only represent one person or group's point of view?

Example:

'This cartoon is taken from the magazine, *Sunday* which is given away free with the *News of the World* – a paper read mostly by working class people.

The cartoon assumes that the woman is "lazy" because she has not dusted the television. This shows that the cartoonist is putting forward a stereotypical view of roles in marriage where all housework is seen as the wife's responsibility.

Cartoons like this reinforce some people's very traditional views of the relationship between men and women, and play a part in preventing a more equal sharing of duties in the home.'

(Julie Harris)

Presenting data: reminders

Have you:–

- Thought about the most effective way of presenting your findings?
- Labelled each table, graph and diagram clearly?
- Included a discussion of how you collected the data, including any problems you had, especially those which might affect the reliability of the data?
- Discussed what your data shows and how it relates to the general aims of your research or hypothesis?

13 Explaining Results

What have I found out?

There will come a point in your research when you have collected your data and are left with the question: 'What have I actually found out?'

Now, before you claim that you've discovered the secret of the universe, think about this:–

Professional social scientists have far more time and money than you. They

- a) sometimes make mistakes in their research
- b) often don't find out anything very new or different.

Let's look at these points in more detail:–

a) It is inevitable that you will make mistakes in your research – anything from unrepresentative sampling to batteries in a tape recorder running out. Of course mistakes affect the accuracy of your results, but they don't often ruin the whole project. In fact, your mistakes teach you a great deal about doing research, and as long as you admit to them, and discuss them in your coursework, the examiner will be pleased that you are aware of what you did wrong. In fact, they are likely to be very suspicious if you make it appear that everything went perfectly.

b) Your research may be mostly concerned with description: the lifestyle of a particular group or the day to day activities of housewives for example. On the other hand it may be attempting to explain or analyse the **causes** of something, such as increasing unemployment or changing patterns of leisure. Either way, you should not expect too much from your research – it is unlikely that you will be able to completely prove or disprove an hypothesis for instance. However, you will be able to collect evidence for and/or against it and make some interesting general observations.

You should be particularly careful about claiming that one thing **causes** something else.

> Example: Your hypothesis is: 'Children who have experienced pre-school education do better at school than those who have not.'
>
> As part of your investigation you ask a number of higher and

lower stream pupils in local schools whether they had any pre-school education outside the home. You find that a large majority of the higher stream pupils had, but only about half of the lower stream pupils. This result seems to suggest that your hypothesis is correct. However, if you think a little harder the issue becomes much less simple:-

From looking at sociologist's work on education you know that parental interest is a major factor affecting success at school. It may well be that parents who are very interested in their child's education are the most likely to send their children to some form of pre-school education, and that their children will also be the most likely to do well in their later school career. So parental interest is a more important **cause** of educational success than pre-school education.

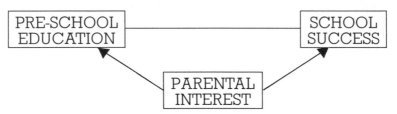

So, just because two factors seem to relate to each other it doesn't necessarily mean that one causes the other.

Exercise 1

Here are a number of sets of two factors which you find relate to each other. In each case can you think of another factor which might be a cause of both?

a) Living a semi-detached house ———————————— Playing golf
b) Reading *The Daily Mirror* ———————————— Voting Labour
c) Being a member of a 'youth cult' ———————— Misbehaving at school
d) Enjoying football ——————————— Believing that 'a woman's place is in the home'.

You should try to explain your findings as your research is going on. This might lead you to change your ideas and methods for the rest of the research. Looking at textbooks might also help you come up with possible explanations.

However you choose to do it, explaining your results needs a lot of thought, imagination, and, quite often, guesswork.

What's explaining results really like?

'I found that there was no straight answer to my hypothesis because it was very complex.'

'I can't really prove that comics and magazines socialise you into traditional sex roles, but there is lots of evidence to suggest that they could if you let them.'

'I didn't reach exactly the same conclusion as other sociologists but neither did I find anything new or startling.'

'I am not altogether pleased with what I have found out. My research has left me with a big question mark because it shows me that my hypothesis is both right and wrong.'

'The more my research progressed, the more I realised I was only skimming the surface.'

'Before I started my coursework I thought I already knew what the result would be: that people under 21 would be less racist than their elders. I now know that this is not the case. I was very shocked at the racism I found among people of my own age.'

'So, I have proved that women are more likely to go on "the pill" than men.'

Explaining results: reminders

Have you:–

- Made sure your expectations of your results are not too high?
- Admitted to any mistakes you have made?
- Thought very carefully about what your results show?
- Tried to explain how your findings relate to your hypothesis, general aims, and other social scientists' results?

14 Writing a research project

How should I go about writing my research project?

- Collect information gradually and be prepared to change your plans in the light of your findings. Don't leave things until the last minute.

- Don't attempt to write out your project as you go along. You will not be able to see how everything fits together until all your data has been collected.

- Keep a diary of your research. Jot down in it everything that happens during your research: what letters you write, how your data collection goes, what books you look at, how you feel the research is going, and so on. Write down the date of each entry in your diary.

- Remember that everything that happens during your research is relevant – uncooperative respondents, people who write silly things on questionnaires, organisations that don't reply to your letters. Writing about these things will show the examiner that you have faced the same problems as other social scientists and are aware that they are problems.

- Write up any work you do as soon as you can after having completed it. If you leave it any length of time you might forget what happened.

- Look after your notes very carefully; try and get a file you can keep all your coursework material in.

- Be prepared to go through different moods while doing your coursework: sometimes you may feel cheerful and full of enthusiasm for the project while at other times you may feel bored and unwilling to work at it – hopefully this mood will pass.

- Eventually you should have a mass of what are called 'field notes' – all the data you have collected as well as notes on how the research went. Now you can begin to plan the final version of your research project.

How should I present my research project?

- Plan your research project before you begin to write it. Draw up a list of headings in the order you intend to include them.

- Write your project in rough first so that your final version will be neat.

- Make your coursework look as attractive as possible: include graphs, diagrams, pictures, cartoons, newspaper and magazine articles, and other visual material. Why not take some relevant photographs and include them? Remember to label clearly all visual material.

- Whatever you include, make sure that it is relevant and is adding something to your project. Don't be afraid to leave material out if it does not add anything to your research.

- You should include an appendix: a section at the end which includes examples of questionnaires, interview schedules, a list of books you used, organisations you wrote to, places you visited, your research diary, and other field notes.

- Don't number the pages and add a table of contents until you are almost ready to hand your coursework in.

- Your coursework should usually include:-

    - why you chose the topic you did
    - why you chose the aims or hypothesis you did
    - why you chose particular research methods
    - how you did the research
    - the problems you had doing the research
    - your findings and how you interpret them
    - your conclusions, including what you have discovered about your hypothesis or the general aims of your research
    - what changes you would make if you repeated the research
    - what further research might be useful to develop your project
    - an appendix

- Why not show your final research project to the people involved in it; those you observed, interview respondents etc? You could also show it to other groups and individuals who may be interested.

How can my teacher help?

- Arranging for the loan of books, cameras, cassette recorders
- Arranging for the duplication of questionnaires, articles, pictures and photographs
- Advising you about, and arranging for, possible visits
- Advising you on possible organisations you could write to

- Giving you information about other social scientists' work in the same area
- Helping you choose and plan your research methods
- Helping you analyse and present your research findings
- Advising you on how to organise, and what to include in, the final version of your research project

Your teacher is probably the most important resource you have, but remember that you are not the only person in the class.

Your teacher will always give you help.

What's writing a research project really like?

'My attitude to the research changed. At the beginning I was very excited about doing the research but when I didn't get many of the questionnaires back I lost interest. At the end it got better because I was looking forward to seeing the end result of my work.'

'My coursework took up a lot of time and I got behind on other schoolwork.'

'I am getting fed up with this research. I don't seem to be getting anywhere and I have not found out any interesting information yet.'

'To begin with, I thought of the project as a chore; just another piece of work I had to do; but by the end I was enjoying it and it was quite pleasing to see it coming together.'

'I feel I can't be bothered to work yet I must. It just seems like I'm always busy – home chores, babysitting, and I go swimming every Friday.'

'It was boring from beginning to end.'

'I think it was the most interesting thing I did at school.'

'My mum threw all my notes away so I suppose I'll get nought.'

15 Putting it all Together

So far we have looked at the various parts of a research project. Now it's time to see how the parts fit together. The following examples show how what you've learned in the book can be put together into a coursework project.

Example 1: Record buying

General aim

To examine the types of records bought by young people.

Hypothesis

Different social groups buy different types of records.

Methods

You decide that your main source of data will be a questionnaire. How will you select your sample? How big a sample can you manage? Are the people you want to select from the sample readily available? With these questions in mind you decide to draw a sample from your own school. One advantage of this is that different age and gender groups will probably be available in the school. You then choose the kind of sample you want – stratified random etc. Which do you think would be best to use?

You now need to classify kinds of music and people. You prepare a list of different kinds of music and try it out on your friends. Does the music they like fit into your categories? This is important because if, say, the term 'soul music' means different things to different people, then the results of your research may be distorted. You also need to classify people into social groups. Gender groups are quite straightforward. Age groups are more of a problem. Take the age group 11–18: how would you subdivide it into different age groups? Next, you have the problem of social class. Sociologists disagree amongst themselves about how to classify social class. It's probably easiest to use the Registrar General's classification but you must be aware of the problems involved. Ethnicity seems fairly simple but there are also problems here (as described in Example 5, pages 92–93).

What about other social groups with might be present in your school, for instance different streams and friendship groups? Do you think it would be useful to identify these?

As you can see, a lot of work is needed before you can even write the questionnaire!

Presentation and analysis of results

One method of analysis is to calculate what percentage of each social group buys each type of record. You can then present your results in the form of bar graphs or pie charts as shown in the following examples.

Age groups and soul music
(percentage that bought at least one soul record a month)

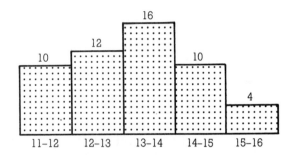

Social class and soul music
(social class distribution of those who bought at least one soul record a month – Social classes 1–5)

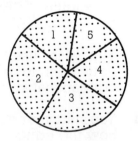

Your results show that different groups buy different types of records. Why is this the case? Maybe some possible answers will have emerged while doing the research. You may have asked people why they like a particular kind of music. Often however, you will have to make guesses based on your results. You will need to use what you've learned during the course and do a bit of creative thinking.

Possible further research

- In-depth interviews with record buyers
- Observation inside a record shop

Example 2: The History of Education

General aim

To investigate changes in people's experience of education.

Hypothesis

Despite changes in the education system people's experience of education remains similar.

Methods

You decide that in-depth interviews are the best way to find out how people feel about their education. You plan interviews with your grandmother, who was at school in the 1920s, and your father, who was at school in the 1950s. You also interview an aunt who attended a private school, and a friend of your grandmother who was at school at roughly the same time as her. You choose to interview the two pairs together, feeling that they will 'spark off' each others memories. In order to get a view of education today you write your own educational autobiography.

You have a list of topics to cover in each interview, but your main aim is to just let respondents talk about their education. Your topics are; 'Subjects studied', 'Teaching methods', 'Behaviour in the classroom', 'Discipline', 'Exams', 'Friends', and 'Rules and regulations'. You tape record the interviews.

You also use textbooks and other books about education to give you a picture of the changing educational system.

Presentation and analysis of results

You start your coursework project with a description of how the education system has changed this century, then explain how and why you chose to study the aspect of education you did.

You present the results of your interviews in two sections: 'Education in the 1920s' and 'Education in the

1950s'. Under each title you use your interview topics as sub-headings. Your educational autobiography follows. The research is illustrated with photographs of the people you interviewed and the schools they attended.

Your conclusion discusses the differences in your respondents' feelings about their education and whether their different experiences reflect changes in the education system. You discuss the evidence you have collected for and against your hypothesis and explain how your sample is likely to be unrepresentative.

Your final task is to show your research project to the people you interviewed and ask for their comments.

Possible further research

- In-depth interviews with long serving teachers at your school
- Investigation of old school records and documents

Example 3: The Supermarket

General aim

To investigate the social relationships in a large supermarket.

Hypothesis

No hypothesis.

Methods

You decide to do a case study of the supermarket you work in on Saturdays and during the school holidays.

Your first step is to discuss the idea with the manager. He is very interested and gives you permission to go ahead with the research as long as he can be the first to see your results.

You use a mixture of methods which you hope will give a balanced picture of life in the supermarket:-

    – in-depth interviews with workers at all levels
    – participant observation while you are at work
    – structured interviews with all workers

You also use company records and publicity material to illustrate your research.

You start with the in-depth interviews as you believe that they might point the case study in some useful directions. They prove to be very difficult to set up because they have to take place during lunch and tea breaks when everyone, including you, needs a rest.

Participant observation takes place over three Saturdays – you observe other staff at work, and make notes on their attitudes to their job, fellow workers, and management. You have to make your notes in the toilet so that nobody will know they are being observed!

The structured interviews have to be brief and fitted in when people have a spare moment.

Presentation and analysis of results

Look carefully at all the data you've collected; do the observational findings contradict or back up the interview findings? How are the results of the strucured interviews different? What were the attitudes of workers to their work, other workers, management, the supermarket? Did different kinds of workers have different attitudes, for instance part-time and full-time, manual and non-manual? What explanations are there for these differences – perhaps you'll have to look at other sociologists' work in text-books to give you some ideas.

The introduction to your final presentation is a general account of the history of the supermarket. You then describe each method you used including how the research went and what insights into the social relationships of the supermarket the method gave. Your conclusion compares the results obtained by each of the methods and discusses how the super-market could be improved in the future.

You then show your research to the manager which is rather embarrassing because it is very critical of him (of course, all respondents are anonymous!).

Possible further research

● Case study of a 'corner shop' as a comparison
● A history of the supermarket using secondary data.

Example 4: Observation of a Pop Group

General aim

To investigate the tensions in an unsuccessful pop group.

Hypothesis

Lack of success will cause a great deal of tension.

Methods

A friend of yours plays in a band. They have been together for some time and have played at local clubs quite regularly. However, no record company has shown any interest in them and they are now thinking of splitting up.

You decide to study them by means of participant observation. You feel that you have to remain 'hidden' because they would not cooperate or act naturally if they knew what you were doing. You already participate in their activities by watching them play, socialising with them and helping them carry equipment.

You observe the group playing at a youth club, at two rehearsals, and at three group meetings, over a period of two months.

You make notes directly after your observations or even during them – this is possible because it is sometimes easy to slip out of meetings and rehearsals. For your first observation you don't have particular issues in mind but notice that the arguments that develop are usually about money, music, the future of the group, or personality clashes. In future observations you use these as headings to note the arguments and rivalries in the group, as well as making general notes on what happened and who said what.

Presentation and analysis of results

Look at your observation notes: how did arguments begin, who started them, what were their causes, how were they ended, would they still have occurred if the group had been successful, or if different people had been in the band?

The presentation of your research findings begins with a history of the group, illustrated by photographs. You also discuss your role in the group, your relationship with group members and how you planned and carried out the research.

91

Your account of the observation is in diary form; what happened on each day of the observation.

The conclusion discusses the stresses and strains of being in a group and uses examples of more famous groups to illustrate points.

Now you have to decide whether or not to show your project to the group. What are the advantages and disadvantages of doing this?

Possible further research

- In-depth interviews with the group.
- An account of the pop business using secondary data.

Example 5:   Racism in Children's Books

General aim

To investigate the place of ethnic minorities in children's books.

Hypothesis

Children's books in Britain mostly ignore ethnic minorities.

Methods

You decide that your basic method will be content analysis of a sample of books. Your first problem is that there are a huge number of children's books and you will only be able to include a few in your sample. Which should you choose – books for older or younger children or a mixture of both; school books, fiction or non-fiction?

You eventually choose to look at a number of young children's reading books and contact a local junior school who lend you copies of the books they use. After glancing through the books you decide to just look at the pictures and count up the number of times that people from different ethnic groups appear. Now you run into the problem of classifying ethnic groups: the category, 'Asian' for example, covers people from many different countries, a lot of whom were born in Britain. You decide to use 'Afro-Caribbean', 'European' and 'Asian' as categories, although you run into trouble when a Japanese child appears in one book!

Another aspect of your research is to look at what people are doing in the pictures; are black people shown doing less important tasks than white people for instance?

Presentation and analysis of results

The results of your content analysis are presented in the form of a table like this:–

Book title	People in pictures		
	Afro-Caribbean	Asian	European
Slippery Soap	8	1	8
Karen's Bike	5	0	16
Out and About	0	0	18
Football	0	0	38
Oliver Twist	3	0	20
Here We Go	0	0	47

(Helen Rowlerson)

You can then discuss these results. What do they show? What explanations might there be for the different number of pictures of each ethnic group? Are there any differences in the tasks the people are performing that relate to their ethnic background? You include photocopies of some of the pictures to illustrate points you make.

The conclusion discusses your hypothesis, as well as how successfully books like these prepare children for life in a multi-cultural society.

Possible further research

● Interviews with teachers about racial images in the books they use.

● Writing to your local education authority asking whether they have any policy on the books their schools use.

● Further content analysis of different kinds of children's books.

Example 6: The Youth Training Scheme

General aim

To investigate YTS in one area.

Hypothesis

The YTS is just a way of obtaining cheap labour.

Methods

You start by visiting the local office of the Manpower Services Commission (the organisation with overall responsibility for the YTS). They give you a list of employers who run Youth Training Schemes in your area. You write to them all, enclosing a questionnaire and asking whether it would be possible to visit them and talk to YTS trainees and supervisors. Quite a few employers reply, some inviting you to visit. However, you are worried that your sample may not be representative as the employers who bothered to reply may well be the ones who offer the best schemes.

On your visits you have problems doing interviews because of lack of privacy, time, and the availability of the people you want to interview. However, you are able to add some useful observational data based on your impressions of the firm's YTS.

You also use some official statistics from *Social Trends* relating to the increase in YTS places, how the scheme affects the unemployment figures and the implications of the two year YTS. You also collect relevant cuttings from newspapers.

Presentation and analysis of results

What do your results tell you about your hypothesis? What other reasons are there for the introduction of YTS? How do the different schemes compare? How many trainees go on to get jobs in the firm where they did YTS? What are trainees views of YTS? What about schemes based in local colleges? You will have to think about these and other questions before you can begin to write the final account of your research.

Your introduction describes the background to YTS, what it is, and how it has expanded. Statistics and newspaper cuttings back up the points you are making.

Your questionnaire results are expressed in the form of bar charts and written analysis, including a discussion of how representative your sample is likely to be.

The interviews are presented in two sections: those with trainees and those with supervisors.

Observational data comes last, including a discussion of how accurate a picture of YTS you think you obtained.

Your Appendix includes a copy of the letters you sent to firms, the replies you received, and a copy of your questionnaire.

Possible further research

- Write to youth pressure groups such as Youthaid for their views and research findings on YTS.

- Interview careers teachers in school.

- Interview pupils in their last year at school about their feelings on YTS.

Appendix: List of Useful Addresses

This list represents only a small number of the organisations which might provide information relevant to your research. You may get other ideas for addresses from your teacher or local reference library. An example of the kind of letter you could write is given on p. 65.

When you write for information remember the following points:-

- Find out a little about the organisation, making sure it is relevant, before you write.
- Try and explain clearly the kind of information you want.
- Enclose a large stamped addressed envelope unless otherwise stated.
- If the organisation you are writing to has a local branch, write to them. They might respond more helpfully to your request.
- Address your letters to the Information Department of the organisation unless otherwise stated.
- Don't be disheartened if you don't receive replies.

General

- Your local council can provide you with a wide range of information on social services, housing, education and the other services they are responsible for.

- The Citizens Advice Bureau should have a variety of booklets and information sheets on a range of welfare, housing and legal issues.

- The Trades Union Congress will give you information on all aspects of employment and industrial relations including race, gender, unemployment and new technology.

    Trades Union Congress,
    Congress House,
    Great Russell Street,
    London WC1B 3L6

- The Office of Population Censuses and Surveys produces official statistics and other information on issues which are of concern to the government.

    OPCS Information Branch,
    St. Catherines House,
    10, Kingsway,
    London WC2B 6JP

Age

Children's Legal Centre,
20, Compton Terrace,
London N1 2UN

Youthaid,
9, Poland Street,
London W1V 3DG

Age Concern,
Bernard Sunley House,
Pitcairn Road,
Mitcham,
Surrey CR4 3LL

Help the Aged,
St. James Walk,
London EC1R 0BE

Crime

Your local police station

National Association of Victim
Support Schemes,
17a, Electric Lane,
London SW9 8LA

National Association for the Care
and Resettlement of Offenders,
169, Clapham Road,
London SW9 0PU

Howard League for Penal Reform,
322, Kennington Park Road,
London SE11 4PP

Education

Your local council: Education Dept.

Press and PR Officer,
Independent Schools Information
Service,
56, Buckingham Gate,
London SW1E 6AG

Department of Education and
Science,
Elizabeth House,
York Road,
London SE1 7PH

Manpower Services Commission
(see under 'Work')

Family

Family Policy Studies Centre,
231, Baker Street,
London NW1 6XE

Family Welfare Association,
501, Kingsland Road,
London E8 4AU

(please send 13" by 9" envelope
with stamps to the value of 24p)

National Council for One Parent
Families,
255, Kentish Town Road,
London NW5 2LX

Gender

Equal Opportunities Commission,
Overseas House,
Quay Street,
Manchester M3 3HN

(send stamps only)

Trades Union Congress
(see under 'Work')

Health

Health Education Council,
78, New Oxford Street,
London WC1

(no need for SAE)

Royal Society for Mentally
Handicapped Children and Adults
(MENCAP),
123, Golden Lane,
London EC1

Disability Alliance,
25, Denmark Street,
London WC2 8NJ

Alcoholics Anonymous,
General Service Office,
PO Box 1,
Stonebow House,
Stonebow,
York YO1 2NJ

Your local Community Health
Council

Housing

(see under 'Urban and Rural Life')

International Relations

United Nations Information Centre,
20, Buckingham Gate,
London SW1E 6LB

European Parliament Information
Centre,
2, Queen Annes Gate,
London SW1H 9AA

Campaign for Nuclear
Disarmament,
22–24 Underwood Street,
London N1 7JG

Council for Education in World
Citizenship,
Seymour Mews House,
Seymour Mews,
London W1H 9PE

Leisure

Your local sports centre

National Association of Youth
Clubs,
Keswick House,
30, Peacock Lane,
Leics. LE1 5NY

Central Council for Physical
Recreation,
Francis House,
Francis Street,
London SW1P 1DE

Mass Media

Programme Correspondence
Section,
British Broadcasting Corporation,
Broadcasting House,
Portland Place,
London W1A 1AA

Independent Broadcasting
Authority,
70, Brompton Road,
London SW3 1EY

Advertising Standards Authority,
Brook House,
Torrington Place,
London WC1E 7HN

Campaign for Press and
Broadcasting Freedom,
9, Poland Street,
London W1V 3DG

Politics

Conservative Party,
32, Smith Square,
London SW1P 3HH

Labour Party,
150, Walworth Road,
London SE17

Liberal Party,
1, Whitehall Place,
London SW1A 2HE

Social Democratic Party,
4, Cowley Street,
London SW1P 3NB

Local Government Information
Unit,
1/5, Bath Street,
London EC1V 9QQ

Population

Office of Population Censuses and
Surveys,
(see under 'General')

Population Concern,
231, Tottenham Court Road,
London W1P 9AE

(see also under 'Third World')

Poverty

Child Poverty Action Group,
1, Macklin Street,
London WC2B 5NA

Low Pay Unit,
9, Upper Berkeley Street,
London W1H 8BY

leaflets available from your local
Department of Health and Social
Security.

(see also under 'Third World')

Race

Commission for Racial Equality,
Elliot House,
10/12, Allington Street,
London SW15 1EH

Anti Apartheid Movement,
13, Mandela Street,
London NW1 0DW

Runnymede Trust,
178, North Gower Street,
London NW1 2NB

Institute of Race Relations,
2–6, Leeke Street,
London WC1X 9HS

Religion

Religious Education Development
Centre,
23, Kensington Square,
London W8 5HN

Islamic Cultural Centre,
146, Park Road,
London NW8

Catholic Enquiry Centre,
120, West Heath Road,
Hampstead,
London NW3 7TX

Church of England Information
Office,
Church House,
Great Smith Street,
London SW1

Hindu Cultural Centre,
39, Grafton Terrace,
London NW5

Third World

Education Correspondent,
Youth and Education Department,
Oxfam,
274, Banbury Road,
Oxford OX2 7DZ

War on Want,
1, London Bridge Street,
London SE1

(send stamps only)

Third World First,
232, Cowley Road,
Oxford OX4 1UH

Christian Aid,
PO Box 1,
London SW9 8BH

Action Aid,
Hamlyn House,
Archway,
London N19 5PS

(see also under 'International Relations')

Urban and Rural Life

Shelter,
157, Waterloo Road,
London SE1 8XF

(send stamps only)

Council for the Protection of Rural
England,
4, Hobart Place,
London SW1W 0HY

The National Trust,
36, Queen Annes Gate,
London SW1H 9AS

Town and Country Planning
Association,
17, Carlton House Terrace,
London SW1Y 5AS

Friends of the Earth,
377, City Road,
London EC1V 1NA

Welfare State

(see under 'Poverty' and 'Health')

Work and Unemployment

Trades Union Congress
(see under 'General')

Confederation of British Industry,
Centre Point,
103, New Oxford Street,
London WC1A 1DU

Unemployment Unit,
9, Poland Street,
London W1V 3DG

Manpower Services Commission,
Moorfoot,
Sheffield S1 4PQ

Major Unions such as the
Transport and General Workers
Union